MW01487309

365
Devotional
Prayers

FOR WOMEN

© 2024 by Barbour Publishing, Inc.

Print ISBN 978-1-63609-744-2

Text compiled from *180 Prayers for a Woman of Courage*, *180 Prayers for a Woman of Confidence*, *180 Prayers for a Woman of God*, *180 Prayers for a Hopeful Heart*, all published by Barbour Publishing.

All rights reserved. No part of this publication may be reproduced or transmitted for commercial purposes, except for brief quotations in printed reviews, without written permission of the publisher. Reproduced text may not be used on the World Wide Web.

Churches and other noncommercial interests may reproduce portions of this book without the express written permission of Barbour Publishing, provided that the text does not exceed 500 words or 5 percent of the entire book, whichever is less, and that the text is not material quoted from another publisher. When reproducing text from this book, include the following credit line: "From *365 Devotional Prayers for Women*, published by Barbour Publishing, Inc. Used by permission."

Scripture quotations marked NKJV are taken from the New King James Version®. Copyright © 1982 by Thomas Nelson, Inc. Used by permission. All rights reserved.

Scripture quotations marked NIV are taken from the HOLY BIBLE, NEW INTERNATIONAL VERSION®. NIV®. Copyright © 1973, 1978, 1984, 2011 by Biblica, Inc.™ Used by permission. All rights reserved worldwide.

Scripture quotations marked KJV are taken from the King James Version of the Bible.

Scripture quotations marked NLT are taken from the *Holy Bible*. New Living Translation copyright© 1996, 2004, 2015 by Tyndale House Foundation. Used by permission of Tyndale House Publishers, Inc. Carol Stream, Illinois 60188. All rights reserved.

Scripture quotations marked MSG are from THE MESSAGE. Copyright © by Eugene H. Peterson 1993, 1994, 1995, 1996, 2000, 2001, 2002. Used by permission of NavPress Publishing Group.

Published by Barbour Publishing, Inc., 1810 Barbour Drive, Uhrichsville, Ohio 44683, www.barbourbooks.com

Our mission is to inspire the world with the life-changing message of the Bible.

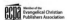

Member of the
Evangelical Christian
Publishers Association

Printed in China.

365
Devotional
Prayers

FOR WOMEN

BARBOUR
PUBLISHING

Make the Next 365 Days a Year of Prayer!

Be still before the LORD.
PSALM 37:7 NIV

The all-powerful God we serve is interested in you. In fact, He longs to hear your prayers. You are welcome—any time—to bring every petition before the King of the universe. Now that's genuine love!

These encouraging daily prayers are especially for those times when you are weary from the busyness of everyday life and your soul is longing for a quiet time of refreshment in the heavenly Creator's calming presence. Although this book isn't meant as a tool for deep Bible study, each soul-stirring prayer can be a touchstone to keep you grounded and focused on the one who hears all your prayers. May this book remind you that the heavenly Father cares about everything you have to say. Go on. . .talk to Him today. He's ready and waiting to hear from you!

DAY 1
Wide Vision

It's such a relief to know that Your vision is wide, Father. You can see from one end of the universe to the other, from every star to every planet to the next breath I'm going to take. You see it all and orchestrate it with Your majestic hand. Because I know Your vision is remarkable, I can count on You to lead and guide. If You can see what's hiding beyond the farthest star, surely You can see what the future holds for me, Your child. Praise You, Lord! Amen.

. . . .

For he views the ends of the earth and
sees everything under the heavens.
JOB 28:24 NIV

DAY 2
Always with Me

Fear comes like a dark shadow to engulf me, but I refuse to become fear's prisoner. As the waves of doubt and unbelief try to wash me away, I remind myself that You are always with me. You are my hope, my light, my salvation. You shine Your light into my situation. You bring peace into my heart and settle me. You speak courage, and I draw strength from Your words. I am comforted by Your presence, and the storm around me roars no more. Fill me with Your peace now.

· ·

Immediately he spoke to them and said,
"Take courage! It is I. Don't be afraid." Then he
climbed into the boat with them, and the wind
died down. They were completely amazed.
MARK 6:50–51 NIV

Choosing Joy, Peace, and Hope

Father, fill my heart with the absolute joy of Your presence today. Fill me with the peace of Your nature and an unwavering hope for my future. Everywhere I look, it seems I can always find a reason to doubt Your goodness and Your omnipotence. Forgive me for the way I have turned from You in moments of uncertainty. I choose, Lord, to start new and to see these complications as opportunities to trust in You. I am confident in the joy, peace, and hope You give me through the Holy Spirit. Your unlimited power resides in my heart. Help me access that power to see Your hand in every situation, from the wonderful to the heartbreaking. Amen.

* *

May the God of hope fill you with all joy and peace as you trust in him, so that you may overflow with hope by the power of the Holy Spirit.

Romans 15:13 niv

DAY 4
The One Who Is

Heavenly Father, today I'm grateful for all You are—the God who is, the God of the living, the great I Am. Your character is unchanging. You are the epitome of perfect holiness and love. Because of who and all You are, I believe and trust in You. Your truthfulness is indisputable, and Your power is established. Not only for the majestic works by Your hand but for the pure glory of Your nature—I worship You today. Amen.

. . . .

Who is like the LORD our God, who dwells on high?
PSALM 113:5 NKJV

Never Anxious

When I'm tempted to allow my thoughts to pull me under the waters of anxiety, remind me that You never want me to be anxious about anything. I don't need to be worried. Today, I spend time saturating my soul in prayer. Help me offer up faith-filled requests to You throughout the day. I will overflow with gratitude and thanksgiving. Thank You that I can share every detail of my life with You, knowing I won't be condemned or judged but comforted. Thank You for Your wonderful peace that surpasses my own human understanding. Thank You for an immediate inner calm in my heart. When my soul is anxious, I will hold tightly to Your promise of peace.

* *

Be anxious for nothing, but in everything by prayer and supplication, with thanksgiving, let your requests be made known to God.
PHILIPPIANS 4:6 NKJV

DAY 6
Mysteries Revealed

I love a good mystery, Lord, but not always when I'm the one who's mystified or confused. When it comes to my life and my future, I want to see where I'm headed. But my life is like a great novel, isn't it, Father? There are whodunits all over the place! And only You know where the story will take me next. I will do my best to calm my heart as Your great mysteries are revealed, step by step. I'll try not to panic when the twists and turns are darkened by night skies. I'll keep my focus on You, Lord. I know You will never fail me. You have revelations aplenty coming my way. What an adventure! Amen.

- -

"He reveals the deep things of darkness and brings utter darkness into the light."

JOB 12:22 NIV

Greater than My Heart

Sometimes I'm wracked with guilt, Lord. I'm not talking about conviction—I'm talking about full-out can't-sleep, can't-eat, can't-think guilt. I have such a hard time taking steps forward because my feet are stuck in the muck and mire of what I've done. Thank You for the promise that You can (and do) set my heart at rest. You are greater than my heart. What a relief! My heart is heavy, burdened. Today, I give it (and this guilt) to You, Father. Forgive me for the wrongs I've done and ease the weight so that I can begin to move into a bright future with You. Amen.

. . . .

This is how we know that we belong to the truth
and how we set our hearts at rest in his presence:
If our hearts condemn us, we know that God is greater
than our hearts, and he knows everything.

1 JOHN 3:19–20 NIV

DAY 8
Grace for Everything

Father, I'm thankful for Your grace—Your unmerited favor to me through Jesus Christ and that special strength You give Your child in times of need, trial, and temptation. If not for Your grace, I wouldn't even be able to approach You. Thank You for extending favor to me: forgiving my sins and adopting me into Your family. And thank You so much for that extra dose of perseverance that You keep giving to me in tough situations. I'm so thankful Your resource center will never experience a shortage. I praise You today for grace. Amen.

. . . .

But he gives us more grace.
JAMES 4:6 NIV

Lord, Help!

It's the simplest prayer, Lord, and I don't say it nearly enough. I was created to need Your assistance. I should always look to You to provide the answers I need, but sometimes I don't. Forgive me when I look to others for the answers You alone can provide. Remind me that the solution is always in my best interest when I ask You. You always wait patiently for me to ask. I know I'm sometimes slow in doing so. Help me not to lean on my own understanding or try to work things out on my own, but to always reach out to You. You have promised, and today I'm asking for Your help.

. . . .

"For I am the Lord your God who takes hold of your right hand and says to you, Do not fear; I will help you."
Isaiah 41:13 niv

DAY 10
Faith Always Produces

God, I look back at where I've been as I'm facing another trial, and I see that You've been faithful. As I trust You now, I know that You have a plan. You always bring me through. Help me not to grow tired. Honestly, sometimes I do want to give up. But then where would I be? I'd be stuck. I cannot quit. I must press on. You are my hope. You will deliver me from this hardship. I will eventually come out on the other side, as long as I hold on to You. My faith in You always produces Your very best for me because You love me and You will never fail me.

* * *

Consider it pure joy, my brothers and sisters, whenever you face trials of many kinds, because you know that the testing of your faith produces perseverance.

JAMES 1:2–3 NIV

Every Step of the Way

Lord, I take comfort in the fact that You've made a way of escape for me, even in my darkest hour. If it's true that You have plans for my future, then I have to believe You have a way to escape today's tragedy in order to take me there. No matter how difficult the road ahead, Father, I trust that You will lead me every step of the way. Amen.

. . . .

*The temptations in your life are no different
from what others experience. And God is faithful.
He will not allow the temptation to be more than
you can stand. When you are tempted, he will
show you a way out so that you can endure.*

1 CORINTHIANS 10:13 NLT

The Inspirational Word

Lord, some mornings I wake up ready to go! I feel rested and energetic. Other mornings, I wonder how I will make it through the day. Remind me that, as Your child, I have a power source that is always available to me. I may not always feel joyful, but the joy of the Lord is my strength. As I spend time in Your Word, renew my strength, I pray. In Jesus' name, amen.

. . . .

For the joy of the LORD is your strength.
NEHEMIAH 8:10 KJV

Amazing Forgiveness

Lord, I come into Your presence, thanking You for forgiveness. In a culture where many experience clinical depression because of guilt, I can know my past is redeemed because of Christ's sacrifice for me. Your forgiveness is so amazing. Although I don't deserve it, You pour it out freely and lovingly. Because You have seen fit to pardon me, I bless Your name today.

. . . .

In Him we have redemption through His blood, the forgiveness of sins, according to the riches of His grace.
EPHESIANS 1:7 NKJV

DAY 14

I Believe

Thank You for the stories in Your Word about people who struggled to believe. At times, I struggle to believe. In my heart of hearts, I know You will deliver on Your promises. You never fail me, God. You are not a man; You cannot lie. But the weight of my troubles puts pressure on my soul. I fight the negative thoughts in my mind. I know I need to let go and not think about them, but continually I have to take those thoughts captive and replace them with Your Word. I need Your help! I will fill my heart with Your promises by reading Your promises. Help my unbelief.

. . . .

Jesus said to him, "If you can believe, all things are possible to him who believes." Immediately the father of the child cried out and said with tears, "Lord, I believe; help my unbelief!"
MARK 9:23–24 NKJV

There Will Be a Future

There's a sense of foreboding that hits me sometimes, Father. I feel like my hopes are dashed. There's no future for me. I confess, I often feel like You've overlooked me and are more focused on others. Thank You for the assurance in Your Word that there will be a future for me. I understand my role, Lord: I'm to see wisdom in my soul (my heart and mind). Though this isn't always easy, I will give it my best shot and trust You with the rest. Amen.

· ·

Why, my soul, are you downcast? Why so disturbed within me? Put your hope in God, for I will yet praise him, my Savior and my God.
PSALM 42:5 NIV

An Enlightened Heart

What a lovely image, Lord! I can have an enlightened heart, one flooded with light. Wow. When the light is turned on, my vision is amplified. I'm able to see the future as a positive place, no matter what I'm going through today. And what an awesome reminder that You've prepared an inheritance for me—a rich and glorious one at that. May the eyes of my heart be completely enlightened so that I never forget You are for me, not against me. Praise You, Father. Amen.

* *

*I pray that your hearts will be flooded with light
so that you can understand the confident hope
he has given to those he called—his holy people
who are his rich and glorious inheritance.*

Ephesians 1:18 nlt

Knowing Where to Draw the Line

Lord, I know it's easier to resist temptation if I've formed my convictions long before the temptation arrives. I resolve to be devoted to You and Your Word. This world I live in is full of compromise—it's expected, even from Christians. Help me know what I believe and what is acceptable in Your sight. Give me wisdom to think through my response to the temptations that may come. Help me know where to draw the line, and help me stay committed to not crossing those lines. Give me strength in my own convictions because of my love for You.

. . . .

But Daniel determined that he would not defile himself by eating the king's food or drinking his wine, so he asked the head of the palace staff to exempt him from the royal diet.

DANIEL 1:8 MSG

DAY 18
True Joy

Thank You, Father, for Your Word, which teaches me how to experience true joy. This world sends me a lot of messages through the media and through those who do not know You. I have tried some of the things that are supposed to bring joy, but they always leave me empty in the end. Thank You for the truth. Help me to abide in You, that I might be overflowing with joy. Amen.

• •

These things have I spoken unto you,
that my joy might remain in you,
and that your joy might be full.
JOHN 15:11 KJV

DAY 19
Living in the Now

Lord, sometimes I feel like I'm living in a strange land, helpless and hopeless because of my anxiety about the future. I give You permission to be sovereign over my past, present, and future. I want to live in the moment. I regret spending time wondering about future events and waiting for certain things to happen so I can be happy. I trust You to work out the details. I will not worry about how You're going to do it but just trust that You will. I put my thoughts on You and Your promises. I choose to live in the now, this moment called today.

* *

*"Be strong and courageous. Do not be afraid or terrified because of them, for the L*ORD *your God goes with you; he will never leave you nor forsake you."*

DEUTERONOMY 31:6 NIV

Nothing Can Separate Me from Your Love

I am loved by You today, Lord, and I will be loved tomorrow. Nothing I do, nothing that happens to me, nothing I go through, will ever bring an end to Your amazing adoration for me. Because I know Your love will remain, I can trust that it will drive You as Your plans for my life move forward. What peace this brings, Father. Thank You. Amen.

• •

And I am convinced that nothing can ever separate us from God's love. Neither death nor life, neither angels nor demons, neither our fears for today nor our worries about tomorrow—not even the powers of hell can separate us from God's love. No power in the sky above or in the earth below—indeed, nothing in all creation will ever be able to separate us from the love of God that is revealed in Christ Jesus our Lord.

Romans 8:38–39 nlt

DAY 21
My Future Is Secure

Every time I fasten my seat belt, I feel secure, Lord. I'm strapped in. Safe. The same is true with my future, now that I've believed in Your Son to save me for all eternity. My spiritual seat belt is fastened tight, but I take absolutely no credit for this. You're holding everything in place. When I come to grips with this truth, I'm assured of something so amazing: I don't have to be scared of tomorrow. I can take bold steps into the unknown. I can see it as an adventure. I'm strapped in tight with You, Father, and You hold the steering wheel. (That fact alone brings the most comfort.) Praise You, Lord. Amen.

. . . .

God saved you by his grace when you believed.
And you can't take credit for this; it is a gift from God.
EPHESIANS 2:8 NLT

DAY 22
Staying Spiritually Fit

Heavenly Father, what I allow to go into my heart is important to You—and me. The things I think about make an impression on my soul. What I hear and see produces thoughts that lead to actions. Help me not to deceive myself by thinking I can rise above the negative input. I will be courageous and refuse to partake of things that I shouldn't. As I spend time in the Bible, thinking about who You are and what Your Word means, it fuels my faith. Help me stay faithful to growing in Your Word. Give me a deep desire to stay spiritually fit.

. . . .

"Don't for a minute let this Book of The Revelation be out of mind. Ponder and meditate on it day and night, making sure you practice everything written in it. Then you'll get where you're going; then you'll succeed."
JOSHUA 1:8 MSG

DAY 23
No More Sorrow

Jesus, Your disciples were dismayed. You told them You were going away but that You would see them again. Those men had walked and talked with You. You were their leader, their friend. How lost they must have felt at Your crucifixion! But three days later. . . Wow! Lord, You turned mourning into rejoicing. Help me to trust in this. Thank You, Jesus. Amen.

. . . .

And ye now therefore have sorrow: but I will
see you again, and your heart shall rejoice,
and your joy no man taketh from you.
JOHN 16:22 KJV

DAY 24
Rejoice in Hope

Patience. You had to go there, didn't You, Lord? We both know that patience isn't my strong suit! But I'm working on it, Father. When troubles come, I tend to panic rather than pray. But today, I turn my voice, my woes, my concerns to You. Instead of whining, I choose to praise. I'll rejoice in the fact that You've got this. You're standing right next to me, ready to offer hope. So, instead of running, I'll stand firm. I'll be patient, difficult as that might be. I'll keep on knocking on the doors of heaven and standing firm in the hope You've given me. Thank You, Lord. Amen.

. . . .

Rejoice in our confident hope. Be patient in trouble, and keep on praying.
ROMANS 12:12 NLT

Heirs According to the Hope

Wow, I love the idea of an inheritance, Lord! It's an amazing feeling to know you're so special to someone that they've left you something wonderful. You, Father, have left the most amazing gift of all—eternal life. I won't need to wait for lawyers to dole it out, either. It's available starting now. It's Your grace that makes this possible. (And trust me, I've needed that grace so many times.) You've somehow made my crooked life straight again. In spite of my mess-ups, You've kept me in the will, Lord. What an amazing Father You are. I praise You. Amen.

. . . .

Because of his grace he made us right in his sight and gave us confidence that we will inherit eternal life.

TITUS 3:7 NLT

DAY 26
Face-to-Face

I am created for relationship with You. Remind me daily that You desire face time with me. Just as You walked in the garden with Adam and talked with him, You desire that same fellowship with me. I will take time for You. I will not allow the busyness of life to overcrowd us. Help me know what You want me to be a part of, and teach me to say no to those things that I should not give my time to. I press into Your presence for an encounter with You now. Just as Moses asked to see Your glory (Exodus 33:18), I too want to see Your glory. Speak to me face-to-face.

. . . .

The LORD would speak to Moses face to face, as one speaks to a friend.
EXODUS 33:11 NIV

Joy in God's Word

Thank You, God, that in Your holy scriptures I find the ways of life. I find wise counsel in the pages of my Bible. You reveal the truth to me, Lord, and there is no greater blessing than to know the truth. You tell me in Your Word that the truth sets me free. I am free to live a life that brings You glory and honor. May others see the joy I have found in You! Amen.

· ·

Thou hast made known to me the ways of life;
thou shalt make me full of joy with thy countenance.
ACTS 2:28 KJV

Pursue the New

Thank You for my new life. I am reborn in Christ, but sometimes I slip back into my old thought patterns, remembering who I was before. I know I should not beat myself up about my past. I am not that old person. I have a new life, new hopes, new dreams. As I study Your Word, help me renew my mind with the truth of who I am now and who You have created me to be. I intentionally put my past behind me. I focus on my future in You. Give me grace to forgive myself, to look past my failures, and to humbly pursue the new.

Anyone united with the Messiah gets a fresh start, is created new. The old life is gone; a new life emerges!
2 CORINTHIANS 5:17 MSG

A Future Hope

Mmm. . .honey. There are so many references to this luscious treat in Your Word, Lord, and I can see why. It adds sweetness to everything it touches. What a revelation, to see that wisdom is like honey. When I approach life's challenges with the wisdom that only You can give, situations are immediately sweetened. And when my situation improves, I'm far more likely to be hopeful about my future. Thank You for the reminder that You've got sweet things in store for me, Father. They're being poured out, even now, like honey for my soul. Now that's a precious promise! I praise You, Lord. Amen.

* *

Know also that wisdom is like honey for you:
If you find it, there is a future hope for you,
and your hope will not be cut off.
PROVERBS 24:14 NIV

Up from the Grave

Hope is a living, breathing thing. I see that now, Lord. I'd always pictured it as a word. A choice. A lifeless thing. But it's not. It's very much alive, quickening my heart even now. Hope boosts my adrenaline. Hope steadies my breathing. Hope shifts my focus. Hope keeps my feet moving. And this hope is alive in me because of the resurrection of Your Son, Jesus. Amazing! When He rose from the dead, He set in motion a hope that refuses to die. What an amazing, motivational gift, Father. Praise You for this hope. Amen.

* *

Through him you believe in God, who raised him from the dead and glorified him, and so your faith and hope are in God.

1 PETER 1:21 NIV

Committed to Your Word

I love Your Word. Your ways are always just and right. I take the path You have chosen for me because Your Word preserves my life. I will walk in the way Your Word compels me to go. Help me follow hard after You with all my heart. Help me keep my heart right so that I always do what pleases You most. When I am weary, help me keep Your commandments. When I am not sure which way to go, light my way with biblical truths. I am committed to Your Word, God. I take it to heart so that I will not sin against You. Help me hear Your voice directing my path!

. . . .

How I long for your precepts!
In your righteousness preserve my life.
PSALM 119:40 NIV

Glorifying God in My Work

God, today as I work both in my home and outside of it, may my attitude glorify You. I am not of this world, but I am in it—and often it has too much influence on me. May I think twice before I grumble, Father, about the tasks set before me this day. I will choose to work as unto my Father. May my countenance reflect Your love to those around me. Amen.

. . . .

And whatsoever ye do, do it heartily, as to the Lord, and not unto men; knowing that of the Lord ye shall receive the reward of the inheritance: for ye serve the Lord Christ.
Colossians 3:23–24 KJV

Boasting in Our Hope

Now, this is one time I don't mind boasting, Lord! I love to brag on You. When other people ask me how I keep going, why I don't crater, I tell them the reason for my hope: You. I sing Your praises. It doesn't always make sense to others, but I love sharing how You're growing me into someone different from who I used to be. Watching how I persevere is giving others hope, Father. Your hope will never put me to shame. I praise You for the hope You've placed in my heart, Lord. I'm bragging on You today. Amen.

* *

And we boast in the hope of the glory of God. Not only so, but we also glory in our sufferings, because we know that suffering produces perseverance; perseverance, character; and character, hope. And hope does not put us to shame, because God's love has been poured out into our hearts through the Holy Spirit, who has been given to us.

ROMANS 5:2–5 NIV

DAY 34
Powerful Words

Father, Your Word is life to me. It brings me peace, security, joy, and understanding about who You are and who You've created me to be. Help me be a student of Your Word. I put Your Word in my heart so that it is with me when I need it most. I speak Your truth, and it silences the words of doubt and fear that Satan whispers to bring worry and anxiety into my life. May Your life-giving words always triumph over any other voice I hear.

* *

Dear friend, listen well to my words; tune your ears to my voice. Keep my message in plain view at all times. Concentrate! Learn it by heart! Those who discover these words live, really live; body and soul, they're bursting with health.

PROVERBS 4:20–22 MSG

Help Me Hope Again

Lord, You make all things beautiful in their time. My life looks so different today than it did before I met You. I know You are working on me. Sometimes it's hard to escape the pain. Tears cloud my vision, and I struggle to find my way. But I know You are making me new. I won't give up hope because Your promises are true. Even though I can't see it now, You have a plan to use me in wonderful ways. I give my all to You. Mold me. Shape me. Help me hope again.

. . . .

He has made everything beautiful in its time.
Also He has put eternity in their hearts,
except that no one can find out the work
that God does from beginning to end.
ECCLESIASTES 3:11 NKJV

Because There Is Hope

I love the word *secure*, Lord. This world is anything but! I'm forced to lock my doors day and night. I get nervous sending my kids or grandkids off to school. There's so much to make me anxious. But in You, Father, I place my trust. In You, we all have security beyond anything the world can offer. We don't have to live in fear. Please replace those fears with hope today, Lord. When I put my head on my pillow at night, I want to rest secure in You. Do a work in my heart and mind, I pray. Amen.

. . . .

"You will be secure, because there is hope; you will look about you and take your rest in safety."

JOB 11:18 NIV

A Hope That's Wanted

This is a hard thing to admit, Lord, but sometimes I simply give up hoping. I don't even want to try anymore because I'm afraid I'll be let down. I can relate to the crippled man in today's scripture. He'd been waiting a long time and probably felt his turn would never come. But when Jesus stepped onto the scene, everything changed. I ask You to renew my hope today, Lord. Give me the desire for change. When You ask, "Do you really want this?" I want to be able to answer with a resounding, "Yes, Lord!" Only You can bring about the necessary changes in my heart, Father. Today, I give You permission to do just that. Amen.

- -

When Jesus saw him lying there and learned that
he had been in this condition for a long time,
he asked him, "Do you want to get well?"
JOHN 5:6 NIV

DAY 38
Putting God First

Father, a glance at my bank statement causes me to shudder. Where does my money go? Am I too concerned with what the world says I must possess to be cool, to fit in, to appear successful? Your Word says that I cannot serve both material wealth and You. I choose You, Lord. Be the master of my life and of my checkbook. I need Your help with this. Amen.

* *

*No man can serve two masters: for either he
will hate the one, and love the other; or else
he will hold to the one, and despise the other.
Ye cannot serve God and mammon.*
MATTHEW 6:24 KJV

A Shield around Me

I hear what they're saying, Lord. They're pointing fingers and whispering, "She won't make it this time. She's going under." Oh, if only they could see what I'm seeing! You have hemmed me in on every side, giving me refuge, even in the midst of troubles. I'm not afraid when I see the efforts You're putting forth to keep me safe. You're like an impenetrable shield all around me. Let those arrows fling. They won't hit me as long as You're on my side. What hope this brings, Father. What confidence. Today, I choose to trust in You. Amen.

* * *

Many are saying of me, "God will not deliver him."
But you, LORD, are a shield around me, my glory,
the One who lifts my head high. I call out to the
LORD, and he answers me from his holy mountain.
I lie down and sleep; I wake again, because the
LORD sustains me. I will not fear though tens
of thousands assail me on every side.

PSALM 3:2–6 NIV

I'm Sure of What I Hope For

Confident. Sure. These words propel me, Father. I want to remain confident, even during the rough seasons. I want to square my shoulders, look my problems in the eye, and be absolutely convinced You're going to come through for me. This takes faith, I know, but You are the author of faith. So that's what I ask for today, Lord. Give me faith to believe for assurance. Give me faith to stand strong when others around me are falling. May I be sure of what I hope for, Father. Amen.

. . . .

"But blessed is the one who trusts in the LORD, whose confidence is in him."
JEREMIAH 17:7 NIV

The Reason for My Hope

I'm so excited that You are motivated to move on my behalf, Lord. Your Word says I need to be ready to explain the reason for my hope, which tells me that You care a great deal about breathing life into my situations. When people rise up against me, I won't be afraid. I'll be ready to give an answer to naysayers, knowing that You're going to move on my behalf. May others be motivated by this hope inside me. I want to be a good witness for You, Lord. Amen.

. . . .

But in your hearts revere Christ as Lord. Always be prepared to give an answer to everyone who asks you to give the reason for the hope that you have. But do this with gentleness and respect, keeping a clear conscience, so that those who speak maliciously against your good behavior in Christ may be ashamed of their slander.

1 PETER 3:15–16 NIV

DAY 42
Exactly What Is Needed

Heavenly Father, You are the restorer of the breach. You bring healing to all the broken places in my life— not because I cry out to You, but because restoration is Your plan. You have a purpose. And even though I want the circumstances to change immediately, I wait for You with patience, with trust, and with faith, because You will bring about what I need. It may not be what I want. It may not happen the way I think it will or the way I want it to. But it will be exactly what is needed. You know me better than I know myself, so I open my heart and ask You to do Your very best.

- -

"Behold, I will bring it health and healing;
I will heal them and reveal to them the
abundance of peace and truth."
JEREMIAH 33:6 NKJV

What Would Jesus Do?

Heavenly Father, sometimes I am a Sunday Christian. How I want to worship You with the rest of my week! Please help me to be mindful of You throughout the week. May Your will and Your ways permeate my thoughts and decisions. Whether I am taking care of things at home or working with others in the workplace, may I glorify You in all that I say and do. Amen.

· ·

Whether therefore ye eat, or drink,
or whatsoever ye do, do all to the glory of God.
1 CORINTHIANS 10:31 KJV

DAY 44
Unexpected Gifts

God, I am grateful for the surprises You bring into my life, even when they catch me unawares and I'm not quite sure how to respond. Everything that comes from You is good, so I must remember to look at Your unexpected acts as gifts from You. Help me keep an open mind when new things appear in my life suddenly. Help me pause and stay calm when it's not something I planned. Remind me to ask if this is a part of Your plan. Give me patience as the gifts You send unfold. It often takes a little time to see and understand the purpose You have in mind.

• •

After all, he's famous for great and unexpected acts; there's no end to his surprises.

JOB 5:9 MSG

Speak the Word during Temptation

Jesus, You were tempted like any other man. You responded to temptation and the enemy with the Word of God after a time of prayer and fasting. You knew God's opinion on any situation You faced. Help me know God's desires for my life. Teach me to use Your Word during the battles I face, especially those occurring in my mind. When the devil tempts me, remind me of scripture. I will speak God's words in every part of my life. With the power of the Word and prayer, I can overcome temptation!

* * *

With my whole heart I have sought You; oh, let me not wander from Your commandments! Your word I have hidden in my heart, that I might not sin against You.

PSALM 119:10–11 NKJV

Restore, Heal, and Cure

God, You are my Creator. You know me from the inside out. When You created me, You made me individual and unique. Every challenge I've had with my health is no mystery to You. Doctors may treat an ailment, but You restore me, heal me, and cure me. You deliver me, body, mind, and spirit. You know my emotional state and what things impact me positively and negatively. You will never give up on me. You will never fail me. Thank You for being there every single time I need You. Reach into me and bring about life-giving health as only You can.

• •

"As for you, I'll come with healing, curing the incurable,
because they all gave up on you and dismissed you
as hopeless—that good-for-nothing Zion."
JEREMIAH 30:17 MSG

Words Are Life

I can only imagine what it was like when You spoke the world into existence. Your words created the earth and everything in it. The sound of Your voice has indescribable power. My Bible is full of Your words. Through Your Word I have come to know You. Each chapter and verse is filled with wisdom and understanding for my life. It is food for my spirit. Help me remember when I read my Bible that Your Word gives me life. Your Word sustains me. And when I pray according to Your Word, all of heaven is backing me up. I rejoice in Your Word. As I go about my day, bring Your Word alive in me. Remind me of Your truth.

• •

"Heaven and earth will pass away,
but my words will never pass away."
Matthew 24:35 niv

Peace Is My Guard

I'm so fickle, Lord. My emotions go up and down as life's circumstances present challenges that seem too much to bear. I'm not proud of this, but when I'm running on empty (or when my peace is waning) it's easy to get caught up in the emotions and lose heart. Thank You for the reminder that Your peace transcends understanding. I don't have to "get it" to be peaceful. I can experience peace even when the storm rages around me. What a revelation, to read that Your peace serves as a guard around my heart. Wow! May it shift my focus to You so that I might live this way all of my days. Amen.

And the peace of God, which transcends all understanding, will guard your hearts and your minds in Christ Jesus.
PHILIPPIANS 4:7 NIV

A Giving Heart

Father, may I be honest? Sometimes I don't feel like serving. They keep asking if I will help with this or that at church. And there is always a collection being taken up. Can't I just focus on me? I have my own needs! But oh, the peace I feel when I lay my head on my pillow at night knowing I have loved with action, with sacrifice. Make me a giver, I ask. Amen.

. . . .

Remember the words of the Lord Jesus, how he said, It is more blessed to give than to receive.

ACTS 20:35 KJV

My Thought Life Matters

When my hope is waning, remind me of this verse, Lord. My thoughts always lead to actions (good or bad), so keep my thoughts on the things that please You. I want to focus on things that are true, not the deceptions of this world or the lies I hear from those who don't know You. I need to focus on noble things—like caring for the poor and tending to those in need. Help me shift my thoughts to doing the right things and remaining pure (a task that isn't always easy in today's society). Lord, may all of my focus be on admirable, lovely things, and may I be a reflection of You to a watching world. Amen.

* *

Finally, brothers and sisters, whatever is true, whatever is noble, whatever is right, whatever is pure, whatever is lovely, whatever is admirable—if anything is excellent or praiseworthy—think about such things.

Philippians 4:8 niv

You Are Rejoicing over Me

How can I remain in the pits when I read a verse like this? I can picture You now, Lord, singing and dancing over me in celebratory fashion. I can imagine the delight on Your face as I learn and grow, as I'm transformed into Your image. It's the same expression I have when I see a toddler making new discoveries or choosing to obey his parents. You're a proud papa, a daddy who longs to sweep His daughter into His arms for a spin around the dance floor. What a blessed daughter I am too. I'm so happy to bring a smile to Your face. Carry on with the song, Lord—may it spill over into my heart too! Amen.

* *

"The LORD your God is with you, the Mighty Warrior who saves. He will take great delight in you; in his love he will no longer rebuke you, but will rejoice over you with singing."

ZEPHANIAH 3:17 NIV

Joyful, Always!

Heavenly Father, I can be an emotional person. But even while acknowledging what is going on around me, I can still maintain my trust in You. I can be unshakable if I have established my dependence on You alone. I refuse to allow my circumstances to make me waver. I will remain cheerful no matter what because my joy comes from You. I will maintain an attitude of prayer, ready to receive from You. And I will live my life in Christ, fully unmovable in my decision to do what You say. As I do Your will, help me embrace a joyful and thankful way of thinking, always.

. . . .

Be cheerful no matter what; pray all the time; thank God no matter what happens. This is the way God wants you who belong to Christ Jesus to live.
1 Thessalonians 5:16–18 msg

Joyful in Hope

God, the longer I live, the more I realize that joy and hope go hand in hand. I have joy because my hope is in You. Thank You, Lord, that as Your daughter, I do not go out to face the day in hopelessness. No matter what happens, I can find joy because my hope is not in this world or in my circumstances. My hope is in the Lord. Amen.

. . . .

Happy is he that hath the God of Jacob for his help, whose hope is in the LORD his God.

PSALM 146:5 KJV

DAY 54
Live Together with Him

I know what it's like to live in a crowded house, Lord. I've had to share space with others, and it's not always comfortable. But sharing space with You? That's a privilege! When I said yes to Your Son, You swept me into Your home and welcomed me to dwell with You. I'm honored to live with You, Father. Thanks for throwing out the welcome mat! Amen.

. . . .

But since we belong to the day, let us be sober, putting on faith and love as a breastplate, and the hope of salvation as a helmet. For God did not appoint us to suffer wrath but to receive salvation through our Lord Jesus Christ. He died for us so that, whether we are awake or asleep, we may live together with him.
1 Thessalonians 5:8–10 niv

Your Unfailing Love

How many times have I slipped on proverbial banana peels, Lord? Dozens! I'm walking along just fine, and then down I go. It brings great comfort to know You catch me when I fall. You're the King of soft landings! You're there for me because You love me. (This I have experienced and know to be true.) Even in my deepest troubles, You've held me upright and put a smile on my face. Father, You must have big plans for me. You've kept me upright so that I can keep moving forward with You. Praise You for Your great love. Amen.

• •

When I said, "My foot is slipping," your unfailing love, LORD, supported me. When anxiety was great within me, your consolation brought me joy.
PSALM 94:18–19 NIV

My Advocate

Thank You, Father, for sending the Holy Spirit. He forever serves as my Advocate to defend and vindicate me. He will always stand between me and my accuser. The Holy Spirit leads and guides me in every area of my life. When He speaks, I will listen because He comforts me and teaches me all things. He directs my steps with peace and helps me make wise choices for my life. He is my inward witness to show me Your best for me. I set my heart on this promise. Help me to diligently listen to the leading of the Holy Spirit.

* * *

"But the Advocate, the Holy Spirit, whom the Father will send in my name, will teach you all things and will remind you of everything I have said to you."
JOHN 14:26 NIV

Serve One Another

God, I have not been put on this earth to serve myself. It is not all about me. Sometimes I forget that! Service is what this life is all about, isn't it? Father, give me opportunities to show love to others today. Make every moment a "God moment." Help me to be aware of the many needs around me. Create in me a heart that loves others and puts them ahead of myself. Amen.

* *

By love serve one another. For all the
law is fulfilled in one word, even in this;
Thou shalt love thy neighbour as thyself.
GALATIANS 5:13–14 KJV

DAY 58

Keep My Footsteps Steady

Your Word is perfect, Your principles long-standing and proven over many lifetimes. You revive my soul with Your wise and trustworthy commands. They fill my heart with joy. My love for Your laws keeps my footsteps steady, and I am safe. Lord, help me discern my errors, and forgive my hidden faults. Keep me from willful sins so that they will not control my life. May the words of my mouth and the meditation of my heart be pleasing in Your sight. Thank You for steadying me in troubled times with the truth of Your Word.

• •

The law of the LORD is perfect, converting the soul; the testimony of the LORD is sure, making wise the simple; the statutes of the LORD are right, rejoicing the heart; the commandment of the LORD is pure, enlightening the eyes.

PSALM 19:7–8 NKJV

Turn Worries into Prayers

Lord, You said worrying doesn't help me. So I look to You. I trust You to do as You've promised. You will perfect everything that concerns me. I bring my worries to You today. I turn those worries into prayers. I will search Your Word and discover Your promises. I will stand firm, speaking Your Word in prayer. By faith, I believe You will make a way when I don't see one. I don't have to know how You will resolve the issue, but I trust that You are at work on my behalf to bring Your very best outcome.

. . . .

"And which of you by worrying can add one cubit to his stature? If you then are not able to do the least, why are you anxious for the rest?"

LUKE 12:25–26 NKJV

Put Me Back Together

Sometimes life brings wonderful and amazing things from You. Other times, I find myself in a battle that I'm losing. On the days I want to quit, I know I can't. I am reminded that no matter how painful the situation or how broken I am, I am committed to You. Even when I feel like I've lost myself, with pieces of my heart scattered all over the place, somehow You find me and put me back together with Your Word. Whisper Your truth to me. I will never forsake Your way! I adhere my heart tightly to Your sayings. Your constant love renews me with the strength I need.

* *

I've committed myself and I'll never turn
back from living by your righteous order.
Everything's falling apart on me, GOD;
put me together again with your Word.
PSALM 119:106–107 MSG

DAY 61

Standing in the Gap

Lord, today I stand in the gap for a friend. I may not know all the details of her situation, but You do. You know the circumstances. You know the need. You know the pain. You know the condition of the heart of everyone affected. Bring peace and hope to this situation. Wrap Your arms around my friend. Show her Your mercy and Your love. Give her words of wisdom, courage, and strength for the days ahead. Bring about Your perfect resolution to this situation. Give me whatever I need to be a support to her. Bless her, Lord, in every way.

. . . .

"So I sought for a man among them who would make a wall, and stand in the gap before Me on behalf of the land, that I should not destroy it; but I found no one."
EZEKIEL 22:30 NKJV

DAY 62

Use Me, Lord

Savior, You laid down Your life for me. You died a horrible death upon a cross. It was death by crucifixion, which was reserved for the worst of criminals. And You had done nothing wrong. You came into the world to save us! You gave Your very life for us. Jesus, take my life. Use me for Your kingdom's work. Only in losing my life for You will I save it. Amen.

. . . .

For whosoever will save his life shall lose it;
but whosoever shall lose his life for my sake
and the gospel's, the same shall save it.
MARK 8:35 KJV

For the Bible-less

Thank You, Father, for the Bible. I can't imagine not having Your Holy Word. Yet there are people who don't have a Bible in their language. They can't read about You like I can. They deserve to have Your truth at their fingertips. They long to know You and hear Your words. Make a way for them to have Your Word, Lord. Bring people together; build translation teams. May all people groups hear You speak to them in their own language. I pray that more people come to know the need for everyone to have Your Word in a language they best understand.

. . . .

I inherited your book on living; it's mine forever—what a gift! And how happy it makes me! I concentrate on doing exactly what you say—I always have and always will.
PSALM 119:111–112 MSG

You Intercede for Me

Father, I know what it's like to intercede for someone. I've gone to bat for loved ones many times over. When I feel passionately about a situation, I'm happy to come out swinging. It's amazing to me that You search my heart and that Your Spirit intercedes for me according to Your will. Even now, intercession is taking place for millions across this globe as You search hearts from continent to continent. Remarkable! There are things happening in the spiritual realm that we cannot see or hear, but I'm thrilled to know You are for us, not against us. Thank You for caring and for interceding on our behalf. Amen.

. . . .

And he who searches our hearts knows the mind of the Spirit, because the Spirit intercedes for God's people in accordance with the will of God.

ROMANS 8:27 NIV

You Meet My Needs

Okay, I'll confess—this is a tough one for me at times, Lord. Sometimes worries slip in. I wonder about the bills. I question Your ability to provide for me. I get bound up with worry as I see my apparent lack. But with You, Father, there is no lack! Thank You for that reminder. I don't want to run after "stuff." You know what I need, and You'll make sure I have enough for each day. That's Your promise. You'll meet all of my needs—emotional, financial, spiritual, and physical. You've got me covered, Lord, and I'm so grateful. Praise You. Amen.

"So do not worry, saying, 'What shall we eat?'
or 'What shall we drink?' or 'What shall we wear?'
For the pagans run after all these things, and your
heavenly Father knows that you need them."
MATTHEW 6:31–32 NIV

DAY 66
Miracle Maker

Lord, here I am again. My prayers today are not for myself but for those I know and love. My heart hurts for someone. She's asked for prayer, and I'm interceding for her. You know what she is facing; You know the miracle she needs. So, God, I'm trusting You to do what only You can do. You are the miracle maker. When no one else can, You can. Show up in this situation. Pour out Your goodness, Your mercy, and Your grace. Repair and restore. The works of Your hands are unlimited. Make a way, even though we cannot see it. Let her see Your marvelous wonders. I know nothing is impossible for You.

* *

"He performs wonders that cannot be fathomed,
miracles that cannot be counted."

JOB 5:9 NIV

God's Word Alive in Me

As I study the Bible, I plant seeds of Your Word in my heart. I pray that Your truths grow up strong in me. Just like a tree grows strong planted by a river, I grow stronger each day with the water of Your Word. I will never fail because Your Word lives in me and Your Word will never fail. When I gave my life to You, Lord, You started a good work in me, and I know that it will continue in me until You return.

· ·

For this reason we also thank God without ceasing, because when you received the word of God which you heard from us, you welcomed it not as the word of men, but as it is in truth, the word of God, which also effectively works in you who believe.

1 Thessalonians 2:13 NKJV

Provisions from God

God, there is no creature on earth You do not see or provide for. I'm bringing praise to You right now for the daily things You supply for me. It is through Your goodness that I have food to eat, clothes to wear, and water to drink. Help me always be thankful for what I have and not emulate the wandering Israelites who, focusing on lack, preferred to complain. Your power is awesome. Thank You for generously supplying my needs each and every day. Amen.

• •

You open Your hand and satisfy
the desire of every living thing.
PSALM 145:16 NKJV

God Always Hears

God, sometimes I'm tempted to believe the lie that You don't hear me when I pray. But You are with me always. You hear me every time I call on You. When Jesus prayed, He acknowledged that You heard Him, and so I acknowledge that You always hear me. Even if I don't sense a reply or feel I have the answers I need, I trust that You still hear me. The answer will come eventually. Thank You for listening. And help me wait patiently, listening to You.

. . . .

And Jesus lifted up His eyes and said, "Father, I thank You that You have heard Me. And I know that You always hear Me, but because of the people who are standing by I said this, that they may believe that You sent Me."
JOHN 11:41–42 NKJV

DAY 70
So Much More

Lord, I'm learning that prayer is not just asking for things. It's not bringing You a list of wants and trying to tell You how I'd like it all worked out. It's truly spending time in Your presence, talking with You and listening for Your reply. Increase my desire to be close to You. I want to know You, experience You, and wait in Your presence. You are my source, truly the only one I can forever depend on. Talk to me. I open my heart. I'm listening. Tell me what I need to hear. I align my heart and my desires with Yours. More than anything, I want to be connected to You.

• •

You ask and do not receive, because you ask amiss,
that you may spend it on your pleasures.
JAMES 4:3 NKJV

By Grace

God, You knew me before I was born. You called my name and planned my way. I am nothing without You. It is by Your might and power that I am who I am. You reached down in Your great love and pulled me up. You planted me on a path You had for me. Nothing can take me out of Your hand. Your grace and mercy go before me. You have led me to the place I'm at today. You never remind me of my mistakes and misgivings. You see me through the eyes of love. You give me success. Thank You for all Your blessings. By Your grace, I am what I am.

By the grace of God I am what I am.
1 CORINTHIANS 15:10 NIV

When God Surprises

Heavenly Father, You give the best surprises. It's taken me a while, but I'm learning that when I ask You for something, You deliver beyond what I can ask or even imagine. Forgive me for the times I've been impatient and ungrateful. I'm sorry. I couldn't see what You were doing behind the scenes. I never should have doubted that You were at work. Your love never fails. Give me grace to wait for Your perfect surprise. Thank You for the sweet, unexpected things. Help me to never take the small things for granted. I trust You and love You with all that is in me.

"Where is your faith?" he asked his disciples. In fear and amazement they asked one another, "Who is this? He commands even the winds and the water, and they obey him."

LUKE 8:25 NIV

Honoring My Parents

Heavenly Father, show me how to honor my parents. Even as I have grown into a woman, Your command remains. Give me patience with my parents. Remind me that with age comes wisdom. Help me to seek their counsel when it is appropriate. God, in Your sovereignty, You gave me the mother and father that You did. May I honor You as I honor them. Amen.

. . . .

*Honour thy father and thy mother, as the
LORD thy God hath commanded thee.*
DEUTERONOMY 5:16 KJV

My Place of Quiet Peace

This world is so loud; it constantly shouts for my attention. My head fills up with so much stuff—things I need to do, questions I need to answer, and never-ending activity. The fast-paced merry-go-round of life won't stop, but I can step off. Help me remember to take time to slow down, to sit down, and to become quiet with You. Nowhere else do I experience the peace You provide. I need time with You every day. Help me to diligently spend those quiet moments with You. Let Your peaceful presence wash over me and quiet my soul.

. . . .

You're my place of quiet retreat;
I wait for your Word to renew me.
PSALM 119:114 MSG

You Bring Me Forth as Gold

I'm beginning to understand the phrase *trial by fire*, Lord. It's not fun, going through the fire, but the result is pretty astounding! I'm like a beautiful golden ring, exquisitely shaped by the master artist. Best of all, the trial by fire purifies me and rids me of the things that drag me down. Your plans for me are so holy, Lord, and so special that they require me to be the best I can be. So purify my heart today, Father. Cleanse me from within. Shape me into Your image. Bring me from the furnace a new woman of God, ready to do Your will. I submit myself to the process, Lord. Amen.

* *

"But he knows the way that I take; when he has tested me, I will come forth as gold."

JOB 23:10 NIV

A Strong Tower

I've scoped out my house, Lord, and know just where to go in case of an emergency. I've picked out the safest room, one where I can wait out the storms. There's another place I love to run to when spiritual storms hit. I sprint straight into Your presence. Not that I have to run very far. You're right next to me, after all. All I have to do is speak the name of Jesus and I'm cocooned in safety. Thank You, my strong tower, for always being a refuge. Nothing can harm me when I'm tucked away in that holy place. Praise You, Lord! Amen.

* *

The name of the LORD is a fortified tower;
the righteous run to it and are safe.
PROVERBS 18:10 NIV

DAY 77

Breathe Prayers

You tell me in Your Word to remain in an atmosphere of prayer. You are always with me, and I want to be listening every moment. Please fill my heart and mind with a desire to stay in communication with You throughout my day. Tune my heart to hear You. May Your Spirit flow through me just like the air I breathe in and out. Let my thoughts be on the work You have for me to do. Fill me with compassion for others. May my lips be ready to speak Your truth in love to those around me, but give me wisdom to know when to be quiet and breathe out a prayer instead.

· ·

"The Spirit of God made me what I am,
the breath of God Almighty gave me life!"

JOB 33:4 MSG

Avoiding Idleness

Lord, I know that You want me to take care of my household. Sometimes I am so tempted to put off my duties around the house, and I find myself spending too much time on the computer or the telephone. Help me to be balanced. Help me to take care of my household and to be aware of the trap of idleness. I know that procrastination is not a good or godly habit. Amen.

* *

She looketh well to the ways of her household,
and eateth not the bread of idleness.

PROVERBS 31:27 KJV

Gently Leading

What a gentle leader You are, Father! I've had earthly leaders who left something to be desired. They pushed too hard, asked too much, or insisted on their own way. But You? You're just the opposite, Lord. You're such a gentle and good shepherd. When I'm weary, You lead me beside still waters. When I'm ready to collapse, You point out places along the path where I can rest. Unlike most earthly leaders, You're more interested in me—in my well-being—than anything else. And yet, somehow, You manage to do it—all for Your name's sake. I want to be that kind of leader, Lord. May I learn from Your amazing example. Amen.

* *

The LORD is my shepherd, I lack nothing. He makes me lie down in green pastures, he leads me beside quiet waters, he refreshes my soul. He guides me along the right paths for his name's sake.

PSALM 23:1–3 NIV

A Forever-After Journey

I love looking through a telescope, Lord, to the vast corners of this marvelous universe. It's an amazing thing to see so far out into space. Oh, but how much farther it is to see all the way into eternity. There's no telescope powerful enough. Your Word gives me amazing glimpses, though, and what I see gets me excited! You've got such joyous things planned for Your kids when we reach heaven. No tears. No crying. Just a forever-after journey with the King of kings and Lord of lords. Praise You for this amazing gift, Father. I can't wait to spend eternity with You. Amen.

• •

For the wages of sin is death, but the gift of God is eternal life in Christ Jesus our Lord.
ROMANS 6:23 NKJV

Steadfast

Father, this verse reminds me of how I feel when I watch the news during a major storm and see those reporters out in high winds. I'm always terrified they'll blow over! Sometimes I'm afraid I'll blow over too—and not just during stormy seasons. Life's circumstances are overwhelming at times and threaten to take me down. But Your Word tells me that I can be immovable. Those winds won't topple me. I know nothing will bring me harm when I walk in Your strength, Father. Show me how to remain steadfast, even when the storms of life thunder overhead. Amen.

. . . .

Therefore, my beloved brethren, be steadfast, immovable, always abounding in the work of the Lord, knowing that your labor is not in vain in the Lord.

1 CORINTHIANS 15:58 NKJV

Back Together Again

Lord, I've cried out to You in my troubles so many times that I've lost count. Thank You for always being there. No matter the number of times I fall apart, You always comfort me in the middle of grief, loss, sorrow, or failure. You are my promise, and I cling tightly to You. You hold me close and save me. Even though my tears blur my vision and I can't see where the pieces of my heart have been scattered, You pick up the fragments and put me back together again. You stand me up, strengthen me, and show me the truth of where I am, as only You can.

. . . .

The LORD is close to the brokenhearted
and saves those who are crushed in spirit.

PSALM 34:18 NIV

Every Good Gift

Father, thank You for the blessings You have poured out on my family. Often, I dwell on that which we do not have. Please remind me to be ever grateful for so many gifts. The comforts we enjoy each day, like running water and electricity, are so easily taken for granted. Thank You for Your provision in our lives. Help me to have a thankful heart so that my family might be more thankful also. Amen.

. . . .

And thou shalt rejoice in every good thing
which the LORD thy God hath given unto thee,
and unto thine house, thou, and the Levite,
and the stranger that is among you.
DEUTERONOMY 26:11 KJV

First Place

I give Your Word first place in my life. I walk in the light of Your Word, stepping where You shine the light of truth, trusting that I am always in the right place at the right time in order to live according to Your purposes. In everything I do, I desire to bring You honor. I want to please You. I refuse to veer to the right or to the left of the path You've set before me. It comforts me, knowing You are always with me. I listen as Your voice speaks to me, telling me the way to go.

· ·

"So shall My word be that goes forth from My mouth; it shall not return to Me void, but it shall accomplish what I please, and it shall prosper in the thing for which I sent it."
ISAIAH 55:11 NKJV

Miracle Words

Lord, how I love Your words—miracle words! Wonderful and true, they are life and healing. Looking back, I see how Your words sustained me. Looking forward, I know Your words will prepare a path before me. As I follow You in all You ask, I will surely find the destiny You have prepared. The opening of Your Word pours light into my soul and gives me supernatural understanding. I choose Your wisdom. I receive Your discernment. Speak to me in the nighttime so that I may rejoice with singing in the morning. I am forever thankful for Your words of life!

. . . .

Every word you give me is a miracle word—how could I help but obey? Break open your words, let the light shine out, let ordinary people see the meaning.
PSALM 119:129–130 MSG

Your Word Makes Anything Possible

Heavenly Father, Your Word is limitless and unbreakable. Thank You, God, for giving me Your Word—Your promises for all eternity. You cannot lie. You say it, and it is so. I choose to trust and believe Your Word above all else. I will grow in faith and stand firm on You and the power of Your Word. It is alive and working in my life. I know that when I speak Your truths and apply faith, the Word will accomplish what You send it to do in my life. You will keep me in perfect peace as I build my life on Your Word. Thank You for making the seemingly impossible a reality in my life.

* *

But Jesus looked at them and said to them,
"With men this is impossible, but with
God all things are possible."
MATTHEW 19:26 NKJV

DAY 87

Simply Follow

Forgive me, Lord, for making obedience harder than it is. I feel like I'm unprepared for what You've asked me to do, but really, I have a hard time letting go. Give me courage to step out, trusting You'll provide everything I need to accomplish the task. You will give me wisdom to act and the words to speak. You will equip me. All I have to do is follow You. I courageously declare that I will do what You've asked. I will step out in faith and trust You to meet me along the way.

. . . .

The Spirit of the Sovereign Lord is on me, because the Lord has anointed me to proclaim good news to the poor. He has sent me to bind up the brokenhearted, to proclaim freedom for the captives and release from darkness for the prisoners.
ISAIAH 61:1 NIV

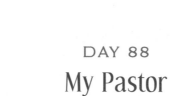

My Pastor

Thank You for my pastor, dear God. He loves You; and he loves those to whom he ministers. Knowing that his desire is to present the truths of the Bible is a great comfort in a world that is full of false teachings. Bless my pastor as he continues to preach Your Word.

• •

And he gave some, apostles; and some, prophets; and some, evangelists; and some, pastors and teachers; for the perfecting of the saints, for the work of the ministry, for the edifying of the body of Christ.
EPHESIANS 4:11–12 KJV

Dreams and Aspirations

Lord, I commit my aspirations to You. I believe that those dreams within my heart were placed there by You and that You have a plan to bring them to fruition. Give me the courage to work toward my goals and not be swayed by the opinions of others. Renew my mind and spirit so I'll be able to test and approve what Your will is—Your good, pleasing, and perfect will. Help me pace myself and learn the things I need to know before I put plans into motion. I will be humble and conscious of the hopes and hearts of others. I will praise You and give You all the glory as we work together for Your good.

* * *

The aspirations of good people end in celebration;
the ambitions of bad people crash.
Proverbs 10:28 msg

My Road, Revealed by God

Heavenly Father, I will stay true to You. You have placed me on the right path. Nothing can take me out of Your hand. I am confident in Your truth. You have plans for me, and those plans are good. You knew me before I was born, and You planned my way. You walk with me and talk with me. When I ask, You answer. When I look to the right or to the left, You whisper gently, "This is the way to go. Follow Me." I am focused. I will stay on course. I refuse to be deterred from walking the road You've chosen for me. Thank You that I don't ever have to walk alone.

. . . .

You're blessed when you stay on course,
walking steadily on the road revealed by GOD.
PSALM 119:1 MSG

DAY 91

Perfect Peace

I confess, Lord, my thoughts don't remain fixed, or still, very often. They ping-pong from place to place, problem to problem, incident to incident. They soar up and then down again. I'm like a kid on a roller coaster much of the time. One of the hardest challenges I've faced in my walk with You is slowing my mind long enough to actually "stay" on You. But I'm working on it, Father. I love this promise that You will keep my mind in perfect peace once I'm able to come into Your presence and shift my focus to You. As the storms around me calm, my trust grows. Help me with this, Father. I want to be fixed on You. Amen.

. . . .

"You will keep him in perfect peace, whose mind is stayed on You, because he trusts in You."

Isaiah 26:3 nkjv

You've Shown the Way

I never have to guess with You, Lord. You're a terrific leader. Your Word, the Bible, gives me great guidance. You also lead me as You gently whisper directions in my ear. You nudge me forward with life's circumstances as well. Any time I'm feeling confused, You're right there, showing me the way. Because You've done this so many millions of times before, I know You'll do it again. And all You ask in exchange is that I continue to walk with You, living as You've shown me how to live, loving those You've given me to love. Now that's a good deal, Father! Thank You. Amen.

* *

He has shown you, O man, what is good;
and what does the LORD require of you but to do justly,
to love mercy, and to walk humbly with your God?
MICAH 6:8 NKJV

The Value of Fellowship

Heavenly Father, I pray that You will not allow me to isolate myself. I need fellowship with other believers. I benefit from spending time with my Christian friends. You tell us in Your Word that it is not good to be alone. We need one another as we walk through this life with all of its ups and downs. When I am tempted to distance myself from others, guide me back into Christian fellowship. Amen.

* *

Two are better than one; because they have a good reward for their labour. For if they fall, the one will lift up his fellow.

ECCLESIASTES 4:9–10 KJV

DAY 94

My Hope Rises

Jesus, Your words in the Bible encourage me. I speak Your Word with my mouth, and hope rises in my heart. I will fight fear with faith, knowing Your glory and truth will overcome the darkness. No darkness can withstand even a sliver of light. I choose to walk in Your light each day. Your gift of resurrection life pushes back the darkness. When I am tempted to allow the darkness to creep into my thoughts, remind me to shine Your light on those thoughts; I know it will expel the darkness.

· ·

Arise, shine; for your light has come! And the glory of the LORD is risen upon you. For behold, the darkness shall cover the earth, and deep darkness the people; but the LORD will arise over you, and His glory will be seen upon you.

ISAIAH 60:1–2 NKJV

Set for Life

God, my life is in You. You alone are my rest. I find peace in Your presence. Thank You for Your all-surpassing strength. When I stumble, You hold me up. I refuse to be shaken by the challenges facing me. When I can't catch my breath, You pour oxygen into my soul. I will not be moved when things don't go my way. I will rise above the disappointment because my future is assured. Because of You, I am set for life. In You, I have everything I need.

. . . .

God, the one and only—I'll wait as long as he says. Everything I hope for comes from him, so why not? He's solid rock under my feet, breathing room for my soul, an impregnable castle: I'm set for life.
PSALM 62:5–6 MSG

Whispers of Encouragement

Lord, You've given me all the answers. They are found in Your Word. When I feel lost and far from You, please remind me of Your truth. Let Your words speak to me as though You were whispering encouragement and direction into my ear. Hold me up with the power of Your Word when I feel defeated. Give me strength when I feel drained by my circumstances. Direct my eyes to the scriptures You would have me read for the answers I need today. You know what I need before I even ask.

* *

"This Book of the Law shall not depart from your mouth, but you shall meditate in it day and night, that you may observe to do according to all that is written in it. For then you will make your way prosperous, and then you will have good success."

JOSHUA 1:8 NKJV

A Long Drink of Salvation

God, it's important to revive my spirit with Your presence. Your Word fuels me. Praise music and moments of worship recharge my spiritual batteries. When I'm tempted to disconnect and close myself off from You, remind me that my health—soul and body—comes from You. I invite You to interrupt my busy life and prompt me to spend time with You.

. . . .

"If you'll hold on to me for dear life," says God,
"I'll get you out of any trouble. I'll give you the best
of care if you'll only get to know and trust me. Call
me and I'll answer, be at your side in bad times;
I'll rescue you, then throw you a party. I'll give you
a long life, give you a long drink of salvation!"
PSALM 91:14–16 MSG

Iron Sharpens Iron

Lord, I find it hard to talk to my friends about areas of their lives in which they are not honoring You. And I certainly do not always appreciate their correction in my life! Father, allow such sweet, godly fellowship between my Christian sisters and me that when truth should be spoken in love, we are able to speak into one another's lives. We need one another. Iron sharpens iron. Amen.

• •

Iron sharpeneth iron; so a man
sharpeneth the countenance of his friend.
PROVERBS 27:17 KJV

Right Words

God, I need Your help. I need a lot of courage for a difficult conversation I must have. I have to tell someone something that's tough to say. I need to be truthful, but it's so hard, God. Please give me the right words. Help me say things in a way that will help and not hurt. Please speak through me. Prepare her heart for what You would have me say. Give me Your grace to do what is necessary.

. . . .

We should no longer be children, tossed to and fro and carried about with every wind of doctrine, by the trickery of men, in the cunning craftiness of deceitful plotting, but, speaking the truth in love, may grow up in all things into Him who is the head—Christ.
EPHESIANS 4:14–15 NKJV

Holding On to Hope

Lord, I refuse to quit! I'm holding on to hope. My hope is in You, my rock and my Redeemer. If I did quit, I realize I would just become stuck. The only way out is to put one foot in front of the other. Give me strength to endure this season. Eventually, it will pass. I must keep pressing on day after day. I will come out of this on the other side. I will look back and see just how far we've come together. I wait with expectation, even if the end is not in sight. I won't let go. You are the answer. You are where I've placed my hope.

. . . .

Wait, Israel, for GOD. Wait with hope.
Hope now; hope always!
PSALM 131:3 MSG

Placing Worry in His Hands

Father, strengthen my heart. Give me the courage I need to overcome fear. I know that You love me and watch over my family and friends far better than I can. I come to You with palms up and arms open wide. I release what I want to hold close. I give You the lives of those I love. I can't protect them or make their lives better. Help me put my worries about them in Your hands. You know their names. You love them more than I do. Give me peace as I let go of them today.

. . . .

*"Who will not fear you, Lord, and bring
glory to your name? For you alone are holy.
All nations will come and worship before you,
for your righteous acts have been revealed."*
Revelation 15:4 niv

Committed to the Journey

God, I want to continue to grow. Let my words, my thoughts, and my choices be pleasing to You. May all that I do be a witness to others. Sometimes it's hard to step out in faith because I don't know all the details. I must trust that You have a good reason for asking me to do this next thing. The secret to change in my life is to give all to You—to let go and let You work everything out for my good. Help me stay committed to the journey ahead, and remind me that others are watching.

· ·

If I am being poured out as a drink offering on the sacrifice and service of your faith, I am glad and rejoice with you all. For the same reason you also be glad and rejoice with me.

PHILIPPIANS 2:17–18 NKJV

Fight My Battles

Father, You've told me who the enemy is. I'm not fighting with men and women. But we are fighting powers we cannot see. Remind me not to blame people when they are used by the enemy. I will keep my focus on You. You fight my battles for me. Give me a courageous heart so I can fight this fight with faith. I praise You in the middle of the battle. You have already declared me victorious. I am guaranteed a win—as long as I stand on Your side, the side of truth!

. . . .

For we do not wrestle against flesh and blood,
but against principalities, against powers, against
the rulers of the darkness of this age, against spiritual
hosts of wickedness in the heavenly places.
EPHESIANS 6:12 NKJV

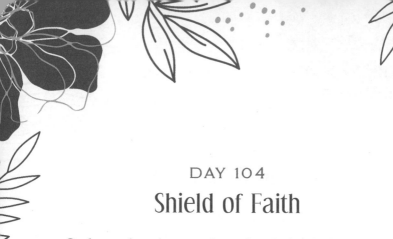

Shield of Faith

God, guard my heart and mind with the shield of faith. I will call on the name of Jesus when Satan tempts me. I will fight against his schemes to ruin me. My weapon is my knowledge of Your Word, promises memorized and cherished. My defense is my faith in Jesus Christ, my Savior. On this faith I will stand. Increase my faith and protect me from the evil one, I pray. Amen.

Above all, taking the shield of faith, wherewith ye shall be able to quench all the fiery darts of the wicked.
EPHESIANS 6:16 KJV

Doubt My Doubt

God, I am filled with a sinking-like-Peter feeling right now. I felt courageous when my eyes were on You. But my circumstances began to roll like billows of the sea and began to overtake me. I looked down; I thought about the challenges. Buoy my faith, Lord, so I don't sink. As I meditate on how You control the wind and the waves, fill me with Your power, courage, and strength. I look to You. Gird me up, and carry me through the rough waters. Help me to doubt my doubt.

* *

But when he saw that the wind was boisterous, he was afraid; and beginning to sink he cried out, saying, "Lord, save me!" And immediately Jesus stretched out His hand and caught him, and said to him, "O you of little faith, why did you doubt?"
MATTHEW 14:30–31 NKJV

No More Exaggeration

Sometimes I'm tempted to make things sound a little better than they are. It's easy to call it an exaggeration. That seems like less of a sin, but adding to the truth is a lie. I don't want to be a liar. Lord, confront me when I speak falsely, and help me to immediately say, "No, that's not true," correcting my mistake as soon as it escapes my mouth. Redeem me from this curse, Lord. Let my words always be truthful.

. . . .

"You are of your father the devil, and the desires of your father you want to do. He was a murderer from the beginning, and does not stand in the truth, because there is no truth in him. When he speaks a lie, he speaks from his own resources, for he is a liar and the father of it."

JOHN 8:44 NKJV

I Know You Love Me

I trust You, Lord. I am learning every day that no one else could ever love me like You do. I look at true human love in my life, and I realize Your love is beyond measure. No matter what comes my way, nothing can remove me from Your hand. Your unconditional, all-consuming love is powerful. It gives me the strength I need to step out in faith, to believe what others perceive as unbelievable. You counted me worthy of Your love, so I know I am precious and valuable.

. . . .

For I am persuaded that neither death nor life,
nor angels nor principalities nor powers, nor things
present nor things to come, nor height nor depth,
nor any other created thing, shall be able to separate us
from the love of God which is in Christ Jesus our Lord.
ROMANS 8:38–39 NKJV

God Thoughts

God, sometimes negative thoughts consume me. I want to think Your thoughts for me, for my life, and for my future. I want to take my negative thoughts and turn them around so that they become positive, faith-filled affirmations. I will pay more attention to what I'm thinking. I choose to think on the truth, on the reputable, and on honorable things. I need Your help keeping those negative, tempting, and worrisome thoughts under control. So I give You authority in my life to help me deal with my thoughts. Help me keep my mind on You.

* *

Finally, brethren, whatever things are true, whatever things are noble, whatever things are just, whatever things are pure, whatever things are lovely, whatever things are of good report, if there is any virtue and if there is anything praiseworthy—meditate on these things.
Philippians 4:8 nkjv

Live an Authentic Life

It takes courage to live in Your light. It takes courage to remove the mask and live genuinely. I've watched the hypocrite and pretender. At times, I've even been one. But I am no longer a daughter of the dark; in Christ I am a child of the light. I can live with nothing to hide—no sin, no hypocrisy, no pretensions, nothing. I choose today to embrace the real me. I owe it to You, God, and to myself to live an authentic life.

. . . .

You groped your way through that murk once, but no longer. You're out in the open now. The bright light of Christ makes your way plain. So no more stumbling around. Get on with it! The good, the right, the true— these are the actions appropriate for daylight hours.

Ephesians 5:8–9 msg

DAY 110

A Beautiful Work

Lord, I read of the woman who poured out a flask of expensive perfume upon Your feet. The disciples did not understand, but You saw it as a beautiful work. Give me a heart like hers. Whatever I possess, whatever comes my way, help me to fling it all forth for Your glory. Let me use it wisely but extravagantly to honor my King. I love You, Lord. Make my life a beautiful work for You. Amen.

. . . .

But when his disciples saw it, they had indignation, saying, To what purpose is this waste? For this ointment might have been sold for much, and given to the poor. When Jesus understood it, he said unto them, Why trouble ye the woman? for she hath wrought a good work upon me.
MATTHEW 26:8–10 KJV

For My Peace

I'm glad that true peace comes from You, Lord, and not from the world around me. People are always telling me how to obtain their version of peace, but it never lasts long. Sometimes I feel so burdened by troubles that it's hard to clear my mind. Then You show up, Father, sweeping away the turmoil in my heart and offering hope that my situation can and will change. My favorite part of this verse is the word *leave*, Lord. You've left Your peace with me. It's not on loan—it's mine forever. What a generous God You are! I'm so grateful. Amen.

* *

"Peace I leave with you; my peace I give you.
I do not give to you as the world gives. Do not
let your hearts be troubled and do not be afraid."
JOHN 14:27 NIV

DAY 112

More than I Could
Ask Or Imagine

I've always loved this verse, Lord! I'm a dreamer with a vivid imagination, as You well know, so I'm always asking for over-the-top things. It's so fun to realize that You are able to do immeasurably more than all I could ask or think. You do it all by Your power, Father, not mine. (This is a very good thing, as I'm limited in my abilities.) Your plans for me include fun, over-the-top things, because You're a creative God. I can't wait to see what You have in store. Looking forward to it, Father. Amen.

* *

Now to him who is able to do immeasurably more than all we ask or imagine, according to his power that is at work within us, to him be glory in the church and in Christ Jesus throughout all generations, for ever and ever! Amen.
EPHESIANS 3:20–21 NIV

Spread God's Peace

Dear God, I pray for peace throughout the world, where there's so much pain, destruction, and disregard for Your creation. Some say peace is impossible—but with You all things are possible! Jesus declared peace for all Your children. We can never look to the world for true peace. That only comes from You. And although peace does not reign throughout the earth, it can reign in my heart. I can be a comfort to others in the middle of life's storms. Give me courage to speak life when things look dark. May Your peace be a tangible gift that I can share with others.

. . . .

"Peace I leave with you, My peace I give to you;
not as the world gives do I give to you. Let not
your heart be troubled, neither let it be afraid."

JOHN 14:27 NKJV

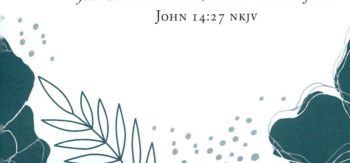

Good-Gift Giver

You give great gifts, Father. Walking with You is like Christmas 365 days a year. Your gifts are more fun to unwrap and last longer than any I've been given. I won't be returning any of them, either! They're hand-tailored, just for me. You know best how to deliver them and how to teach me to use them. If I have any problems, I go straight to the owner's manual (Your Word) for direction. Oh, how I've loved discovering all of these gifts, Lord. Thank You for entrusting them to me. I promise to use them for You. Amen.

* *

"Which of you, if your son asks for bread, will give him a stone? Or if he asks for a fish, will give him a snake? If you, then, though you are evil, know how to give good gifts to your children, how much more will your Father in heaven give good gifts to those who ask him!"

MATTHEW 7:9–11 NIV

Joyful Regardless of Circumstances

Lord, there are days when I can't help but rejoice in what You are doing. But many times the daily grind is just rather humdrum. There is nothing to rejoice about, much less give thanks for! Or is there? Help me, Father, to be joyful and thankful every day. Each day is a gift from You. Remind me of this truth today, and give me a joyful, thankful heart, I ask. Amen.

. . . .

Rejoice evermore. Pray without ceasing.
In every thing give thanks: for this is the
will of God in Christ Jesus concerning you.
1 THESSALONIANS 5:16–18 KJV

As My Soul Prospers

I've walked through dark seasons in the past, and You've seen me through, Lord. There were times when my heart was so broken, I wondered if it would ever heal. My dark days even affected my health, setting me on a downward spiral of sorts. It's hard to believe I've come so far. I thank You for the healing work You've done inside of me, Father, and I look ahead with excitement. When my heart is healthy and whole (i.e., prosperous), my body will follow suit. I can walk with renewed optimism, which greatly affects my health. I want to be completely whole in You, Lord. Amen.

* *

Dear friend, I pray that you may enjoy good health and that all may go well with you, even as your soul is getting along well.

3 JOHN 1:2 NIV

Eternal Life: the Ultimate Gift

So many people in this world are quick to cut me down, Lord. They pass judgment. They bring condemnation. But not You. You're the last one to chop me to bits. In fact, You went out of Your way to do the opposite! Through the gift of Your Son, You've saved me. Sure, You want me to live a godly life. Jesus showed me how to do that—through His actions, His words, His love for others. May I be ever grateful for the ultimate gift from the God of the universe. Amen.

. . . .

For God did not send his Son into the world to condemn the world, but to save the world through him.

JOHN 3:17 NIV

Morning Comes
after the Storm

Father, You know the storms in my life, past and present. You know the one storm weighing heavily on my mind right now. The storm often feels stronger, more powerful, at night. My mind is flooded with negative thoughts, pouring in like ocean water that threatens to sink a ship. But You, my God, are my peace and my calm in the storm. I turn my face to You. I remember the times You took care of the storms of the past. Give me grace to navigate this storm as well. The morning will come and the storm will be no more. I rest in Your loving arms, safe and secure.

* *

Let the morning bring me word of your unfailing love, for I have put my trust in you.
PSALM 143:8 NIV

Increase and Wealth

Father, as Your child, I want to be able to give to every good work. I want to be successful in business and fruitful. You have given me the ability to produce wealth. Lord, bless my work and make everything I put my hand to become a blessing in my life and in others' lives. I study Your Word to learn Your ways. I lean into Your Holy Spirit and receive Your wisdom so that I make good and godly choices. Lead me in the way I should go. Show me the path You've set before me to bring honor and glory to You in my profession.

· ·

But remember the LORD your God, for it is he who gives you the ability to produce wealth, and so confirms his covenant, which he swore to your ancestors, as it is today.

DEUTERONOMY 8:18 NIV

Every Good and Perfect Gift

Sometimes I forget, Lord. I forget that my belongings didn't really come from a store. My income doesn't really come from an employer. My home doesn't really come from a bank or mortgage company. All good things come from You. If it's good, if it's for my benefit, it's all You, Father. And it's all because of Your great love for us, Your kids. You desire to meet every need. May we never forget that our efforts, though good, would never be enough if not for Your provision and Your great love. Praise You, Lord. Amen.

. . . .

Whatever is good and perfect is a gift
coming down to us from God our Father,
who created all the lights in the heavens.
He never changes or casts a shifting shadow.
JAMES 1:17 NLT

A Meek and Quiet Spirit

God, in Your economy, a meek and quiet spirit is worth more than gold. It is not corruptible. It is eternal. Give me such a spirit. Make me a better listener, I pray. Set a guard over my tongue at times when I should not speak. Teach me to walk humbly with You, Father, and to serve people in Your name. A gracious, godly spirit is what You desire to see in me. Amen.

* * *

Whose adorning let it not be that outward adorning of plaiting the hair, and of wearing of gold, or of putting on of apparel; but let it be the hidden man of the heart, in that which is not corruptible, even the ornament of a meek and quiet spirit, which is in the sight of God of great price.

1 Peter 3:3–4 KJV

DAY 122
Every Need Met

Oh, how I love the word *every*, Lord. You don't just want to meet my financial needs. You don't just long to meet my physical needs. You're not going to stop until *every* need is met. What peace this brings! When my needs are emotional, You're there. When I'm in need of provision, You've got it covered. There's not a need I could name that You haven't already provided for. Wow. It boggles my mind when I think about the "everys" in my life. You've got 'em, Lord, and I'm so grateful. Amen.

. . . .

And my God will meet all your needs according
to the riches of his glory in Christ Jesus.
PHILIPPIANS 4:19 NIV

Prospering above the Circumstances

So many times, Lord, I live *under* my circumstances. I let them weigh me down. They dictate whether I move forward. Many times, I remain frozen in place, convinced there's no point in trying. You've asked me to live *above* my circumstances, not below them. With Your help, I can actually soar as free as an eagle. What a hopeful image that paints in my mind! Instead of allowing my challenges to cause weariness, I'll mount up with wings energized by Your Spirit—and off I'll go, stronger than ever. Thank You for lifting me, Lord. Amen.

But those who hope in the LORD will renew their strength. They will soar on wings like eagles; they will run and not grow weary, they will walk and not be faint.

ISAIAH 40:31 NIV

Shine the Light in My Community

There are dark forces at work in our schools, on our streets, and in our homes. I confront the enemy in the name of Jesus. Shine the light of Your glory and goodness into our community. Let Your light illuminate those who give way to evil. Let Your truth spring forth and eliminate the darkness. Protect and keep our first responders as they help us. Keep us safe from harm. You have overcome this world, Jesus. Give me the heart to intercede for others and the courage to protect the weak. Bring many of us believers together to stand against the darkness!

. . . .

The night is far spent, the day is at hand.
Therefore let us cast off the works of darkness,
and let us put on the armor of light.
ROMANS 13:12 NKJV

Powerful Encourager

Lord, I am grateful for the wonderful community You've given me. I can count on them to be there for me when I need support. What a blessing to have authentic people to do life with! They speak life and grace into my life. And they also give me opportunity to do the same for them. Help me be a powerful encourager for others. Bring people across my path who need to hear Your Word. Speak to them through me. Help me be open to receive Your truth and wisdom from those You've placed in my life.

* *

And you must show mercy to those whose faith is wavering. Rescue others by snatching them from the flames of judgment. Show mercy to still others, but do so with great caution, hating the sins that contaminate their lives.

JUDE 1:22–23 NLT

A Witness in My Community

Lord, there are so many people in my community who either don't care about You or who think they will please You by their own merit; but several of them don't truly know You. I ask You to open doors so I may witness to them. My prayer is that many will come to You.

• •

But whoso hath this world's good, and seeth his brother have need, and shutteth up his bowels of compassion from him, how dwelleth the love of God in him?
1 JOHN 3:17 KJV

God's Promise to Do Amazing Things

God, forgive me for my unbelief. Sometimes circumstances surround me, and I am tempted to think You've forgotten me. But You would never abandon me. I remember the many times before when You rescued me. You showed up and delivered me. You've promised to do amazing things in my life. I am ready for a "suddenly"—a big surprise that will amaze me. I believe You will do abundantly above all I can ask or think. Help me wait with patience for Your timing. I praise You today, in advance, knowing something truly wonderful is on its way.

* *

"Look at the nations and watch—and be utterly amazed.
For I am going to do something in your days that
you would not believe, even if you were told."

HABAKKUK 1:5 NIV

An Eternal Perspective

When people think of the word *prosper*, their thoughts often shift to money, lottery tickets, gold coins, jewels, fancy clothes, luxury vehicles, and so on. But You are changing our thinking about this word, Lord, and I love it. You're giving us an eternal perspective. We can't take money with us when we die. Neither can we take fine jewels nor any of the other things that the world considers prosperous. Instead of focusing on those things, today I ask that You give me an eternal perspective. Silver and gold have I none. (Well, very little anyway.) But I have a heavenly perspective that is giving me courage to walk into tomorrow with confidence. Praise You, Father! Amen.

• •

Then Peter said, "Silver or gold I do not have,
but what I do have I give you. In the name
of Jesus Christ of Nazareth, walk."
ACTS 3:6 NIV

All Hope and Peace

Of all the ways You promise to prosper me, Lord, this is one of my favorites. You are the God of all hope and peace. Wow. What good would it do to have everything I'd ever wished for, everything I'd ever dreamed of, if I didn't have hope and peace? Those two things are critical for a prosperous life. And You don't just dole out hope by the teaspoonful, Father. You pour it over me like an ocean wave! I can overflow, Lord, as I trust in You. Today, I choose to do just that. Amen.

. . . .

May the God of hope fill you with all joy and peace
as you trust in him, so that you may overflow
with hope by the power of the Holy Spirit.
ROMANS 15:13 NIV

DAY 130
God's Decree

God, I refuse to give up! I've been waiting, pressing in, asking, and trusting that everything You've promised will occur. Thank You for the joy and the strength You've given me to endure this season. Thank You for the small things that are bringing about Your purpose and plans. I agree with Your Word. All that You've promised is on its way. Even now, I believe blessings are flowing into my life. Your goodness will overtake me. I give You praise today for the overflow.

"Things are going to happen so fast your head will swim, one thing fast on the heels of the other. You won't be able to keep up. Everything will be happening at once—and everywhere you look, blessings! Blessings like wine pouring off the mountains and hills."

AMOS 9:13 MSG

Supernatural Strength

It's fascinating to think about, Lord. Your plans for my life are fully in place, even when I'm exhausted, even when I don't feel like I can put one foot in front of the other. After all, I reach the end of myself pretty quickly, as You well know. I hit a wall. During those times, I can't think clearly, can't move forward. Then You come along. You miraculously give me energy. It comes on me in a supernatural way and even surprises me. With Your strength, I'm able to do more than ever before. Or, I should say that You're able to do more through me. Today, I give You my weariness. I ask You to breathe on me, Holy Spirit, and energize me. Make me a vibrant channel You can flow through. I submit myself to that process. Amen.

. . . .

He gives strength to the weary and
increases the power of the weak.
ISAIAH 40:29 NIV

DAY 132

The Gift of Salvation

Dear Father, thank You for the gift of salvation, for sending Your only Son to be a sacrifice for all people, even those who didn't want Him. I am in awe of Your mercy extended to me. It is incredible to think that I am a daughter of God. Thank You, Jesus, that You didn't walk away from the cross but laid down Your life for me. Thank You, Holy Spirit, for drawing me to this greatest of gifts. My life is forever changed. In Christ's name, amen.

. . . .

For the grace of God has appeared
that offers salvation to all people.

TITUS 2:11 NIV

Fruit of the Spirit

I see how it is, Father—You want to prosper me from the inside out. What good would it do to lavish gifts on me if my heart wasn't in the right place? I would be like a spoiled child, demanding favors but never checking my attitude. Instead, You prosper my soul. You teach me how to live in peace. In joy. Exhibiting kindness, even to those who've hurt me. You prosper me by showing me how to remain faithful, even when I don't feel like it. And You're teaching me self-control every step of the way. I love prospering from the inside out, Lord. Thank You! Amen.

But the fruit of the Spirit is love, joy, peace, forbearance, kindness, goodness, faithfulness, gentleness and self-control. Against such things there is no law.

GALATIANS 5:22–23 NIV

An Earnest Reward

I've never been much for dieting, Lord. It's never fun to sacrifice things I love. Oh, but the rewards can be amazing. It's so much fun to look at before-and-after photos when I've dropped a few pounds. Is that how You feel sometimes, Lord? Do You look at my spiritual before-and-after photos and smile? (I hope I'm progressing in the right direction!) The rewards of seeking You are mine for the taking, but I don't serve You for what I can get out of it. I continue to grow in my relationship with You, Father, because I adore You. I want to please You in all that I do. Amen.

* *

And it is impossible to please God without faith.
Anyone who wants to come to him must
believe that God exists and that he rewards
those who sincerely seek him.
HEBREWS 11:6 NLT

A Joyous Celebration

Father, every day can be a celebration when I walk in relationship with You! With my eyes tipped upward toward You, how can my heart help but sing? My focus on You brings joy. It brings peace, even when things around me are swirling. And if I need any reminders of what it's like to live in holy celebration, all I need to do is look around at nature. The very mountains are singing, even now. Trees are clapping their hands in praise. I join them in bringing honor to Your name, Father. Amen.

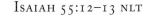

"You will live in joy and peace. The mountains and hills will burst into song, and the trees of the field will clap their hands! Where once there were thorns, cypress trees will grow. Where nettles grew, myrtles will sprout up. These events will bring great honor to the LORD's name; they will be an everlasting sign of his power and love."

ISAIAH 55:12–13 NLT

Perfecting Every Concern

Father, You know the weight I carry in my mind. You know all my thoughts. Help me rise above the thoughts that pervade my mind and influence my heart. Your mercy and love for me endure forever. They will never run out. You are at work in my life perfecting every single concern I have. You work all things out for my good. I turn my eyes to Your Word. I will put Your Word in my heart and trust You, that every word, every promise You have made, will occur at the exact time You've purposed. I wait with patience.

. . . .

The Lord will perfect that which concerns
me; Your mercy, O Lord, endures forever;
do not forsake the works of Your hands.

Psalm 138:8 nkjv

His Spirit in Me!

Thank You, Jesus, for my salvation. I never have to worry about whether I am really a Christian. No one can ever convince me otherwise. The same Spirit that raised You from the dead resides in me. That power is available to me, and I lean into it. The Holy Spirit is working within me. He helps me with daily challenges and teaches me to pray. I am empowered to serve God and do His will. I am a part of God's plan on the earth. His Spirit operates and flows through me even now.

* *

And if the Spirit of him who raised Jesus from the dead is living in you, he who raised Christ from the dead will also give life to your mortal bodies because of his Spirit who lives in you.
ROMANS 8:11 NIV

A Father

God, help me remember that You're my Father. A heavenly Father—one who has unlimited resources and power and one who has infinitely more love than any great earthly dad. When Satan tempts me to view You with suspicion, help me remember that his goal is my utter destruction. Lord, fill my heart with the truth that You love me perfectly and have only the best in mind for me. In fact, You want to embrace me, bless me, and give me heaven as my inheritance. What a wonderful Father You are! Amen.

. . . .

As a father has compassion on his children, so the Lord has compassion on those who fear him.

PSALM 103:13 NIV

The Oil of Blessing

I get it, Lord. One of the ways You want to prosper me is to teach me to walk in harmony with others. When I choose to live this way, the benefits are as precious as fine oil. (I can almost smell it now!) It's not always easy to get along with folks (even inside the walls of my local church), but I love the idea that our unity causes a sweet-smelling fragrance that others will witness and want for themselves. I'm so grateful for Your oil of blessing, Father. Thank You for showing me how to bring honor to Your name through my relationships. Amen.

. . . .

For harmony is as precious as the anointing oil that was poured over Aaron's head, that ran down his beard and onto the border of his robe.

PSALM 133:2 NLT

Prospering:
a Blessed Outcome

What a lesson this verse has been to me, Lord. I'm so quick to ask for Your blessings, but not as quick to seek Your kingdom first. Usually, it's my kingdom I'm after! My desires and my will are usually top priority. Today, I acknowledge that and ask for Your forgiveness. From now on, Father, may Your desires be mine as well. As I run hard after You, after Your will, I know that blessings will come. You desire to prosper me by meeting every need. But my motivation will be for You, Lord. Thanks for the timely reminder. Amen.

* *

"But seek first his kingdom and his righteousness, and all these things will be given to you as well."
MATTHEW 6:33 NIV

Let Others See You in Me

Heavenly Father, today I build myself up in my most holy faith, praying in the Spirit as You speak to my heart. Help me recognize Your truth and turn away from the enemy's attempts to deceive me. Give me a spirit of discernment. Give me words to say in every situation so that I may be a witness to others of Your goodness and love. Thank You for Your power and strength to embrace those things that grow my faith. Let others see You in me today.

. . . .

But you, dear friends, must build each other up in your most holy faith, pray in the power of the Holy Spirit, and await the mercy of our Lord Jesus Christ, who will bring you eternal life. In this way, you will keep yourselves safe in God's love.

JUDE 20–21 NLT

DAY 142

Filled with Contentment

Sometimes my attitude is so "poor me" that I even get sick, Father. I keep thinking that if only I could have this or that, life would be easier. I know I'm missing out on a truly abundant life by whining so much, and I ask You to forgive me. Fill me with contentment. Amen.

• •

Not that I speak in respect of want:
for I have learned, in whatsoever
state I am, therewith to be content.
PHILIPPIANS 4:11 KJV

Prospering in the Details

I don't always remember that all things work together for good. Sometimes I get lost in the details, in the nitty-gritty. Oh, but You've reminded me that I can prosper, even in the minutia. When the day is overwhelmingly busy. When the car breaks down. When the kids won't stop fighting. When the boss is pushing me to recheck my work. Even then, Lord, You're there. Your plan to bring prosperity to my life often takes me to places where I'm inundated with details. But there You are, Father, in the midst of them all. How grateful I am! Amen.

. . . .

And we know that in all things God works for the good of those who love him, who have been called according to his purpose.
ROMANS 8:28 NIV

A Very Full Cup

I know the age-old question, Lord: Do you see the glass as half-empty or half-full? My answer to this question determines how I view the situations I face. Oh, how I love the idea that Your plans to prosper me include a cup that's overflowing with blessings. I won't be looking for it at the bank, Father, but rather in the tiniest details of my life. You have blessed me with friends, mentors, a job, health, and so many other things. You meet my every need, Father. I am well taken care of. Thank You for filling my cup to the top, Lord. Amen.

• •

LORD, you alone are my inheritance,
my cup of blessing.
PSALM 16:5 NLT

All Hope in Him

Today, I place all my hope in You, God. I am learning that true peace can only come from You. I cannot depend on resting when a problem is resolved, because often more problems are just around the corner. It does me no good to worry, so forgive me when I do. Help me stand firm in my confidence, knowing *You* are my hope. I am strong and courageous when I rest in Your holy hand. You work all things together for my good. Because of Your unfailing love, all power and authority belong to You. You have the final say regarding everything that concerns me. I will not let go of You. You are where my hope comes from.

* *

*"Power belongs to you, God, and with
you, Lord, is unfailing love."*
PSALM 62:11–12 NIV

Big-Picture Focus

Lord, each day that I have breath in my lungs is a gift from You. Forgive me for the times when my perspective has been on the problems I face. Help me make every minute count. Help me step back and enjoy the precious times You give me, with You and with those I love. Give me a big-picture focus. Let me look deeply at the things that really matter and gloss over those that don't. Reveal to me the things that I need to know by Your Spirit.

"Eye has not seen, nor ear heard, nor have entered into the heart of man the things which God has prepared for those who love Him." But God has revealed them to us through His Spirit. For the Spirit searches all things, yes, the deep things of God.

1 CORINTHIANS 2:9–10 NKJV

A Perfect Place

Creator God, I wish there weren't diseases in our world. Those tiny microbes that infiltrate the immune system are responsible for so much pain and grief. Although sickness was not present in the Garden of Eden—that perfect place You intended for us—it is a part of this life now, a consequence of the curse under which our world suffers. But someday, You'll create a new earth, and I know bacteria won't stand a chance there. I look forward to that, Father God, for then the world will once again be "very good." Amen.

. . . .

Now I saw a new heaven and a new earth, for the first heaven and the first earth had passed away.
REVELATION 21:1 NKJV

DAY 148
I Trust You

So many things have happened in my life that I don't understand. I've been angry, frightened, and wanted answers. But today, I choose to trust You, Lord. With all my heart, I choose to acknowledge You. You know what You're doing. My life is in Your hands. I don't have to know why. I want the details, but if You decide I don't need them, then I submit to You. I let go of it all. Courageously, I step out in faith, believing You are leading me toward the best outcome. You will show me the way to go, and I am determined to follow You.

· ·

Trust in the LORD with all your heart and lean not on your own understanding; in all your ways submit to him, and he will make your paths straight.

PROVERBS 3:5–6 NIV

Blessed Assurance

Heavenly Father, my salvation is a gift—something I could never earn. It's a treasure given freely with no strings attached. It is mine and can never be taken from me. Nothing can separate me from Your love. Forgive me for the times that I doubted my salvation or thought it was something I needed to achieve or win. Thank You for believing in me, trusting me with Your love. I can stand in confidence each day knowing that I am saved and that I belong to You. My salvation is assured.

. . . .

And by this we know that we are of the truth,
and shall assure our hearts before Him. For if our
heart condemns us, God is greater than our heart,
and knows all things. Beloved, if our heart does not
condemn us, we have confidence toward God.

1 John 3:19–21 NKJV

Freed from Death

I take courage today knowing I belong to the one who raised Christ from the dead. All power and dominion belong to You. Because of Your willingness to give Your one and only Son, and His willingness to die for me, I have the opportunity to live my life in You. You have given me eternal life. I am forever restored to relationship with You. And eternity begins now. I don't have to wait for heaven; I have forever to spend with You. Death could not hold Jesus, and it cannot hold me. I have been freed from the grave.

. . . .

"But God raised him from the dead, freeing him from the agony of death, because it was impossible for death to keep its hold on him."

ACTS 2:24 NIV

Living a God-Fashioned Life

You know I have struggled to put the past behind me. My old nature, before Christ, still tries to hold on to me. I no longer want that life. You have made me new. And I want, more than anything, to live my life fashioned after You. Thank You for seeing me as that new creature. I will become a person who accurately represents You. Give me courage to give up the excuses and get rid of what doesn't please You. Today, I take off the old and walk away.

. . . .

That old way of life has to go. It's rotten through and through. Get rid of it! And then take on an entirely new way of life—a God-fashioned life, a life renewed from the inside and working itself into your conduct as God accurately reproduces his character in you.

EPHESIANS 4:22–24 MSG

DAY 152

His Favor, Always

Heavenly Father, because I am Your child, I am blessed. Pour out Your favor on me. Forgive me for the times You've prepared a blessing and I've gottten in the way. Forgive me for trying to make things happen all by myself—in my timing instead of Yours. Give me ears to hear wisdom when You speak. I will listen to those You've placed in my life to mentor me. I choose to be pliable and moldable; I don't want to be stiff and inflexible to Your will. I choose Your way and not my own. My plans are big, but in no way do they compare to Yours. You saved me. May Your favor rest on me all the days of my life.

*And Esther obtained favor in
the sight of all who saw her.*
ESTHER 2:15 NKJV

DAY 153
Internal Clocks

Heavenly Father, it seems like every person has an internal rhythm seemingly permanently set to a certain time of the day. There are early birds and night owls and middle-of-the-day people. Not many of us are successful in changing our internal clock, Lord. Maybe You wanted to create humans with varying peak hours of energy. It would be a pretty boring world if we all fizzled out at the same time each day. Thank You for the variety You have provided in all of us. Amen.

. . . .

To declare Your lovingkindness in the morning,
and Your faithfulness every night.
PSALM 92:2 NKJV

DAY 154

Listening to God's Direction

Father, thank You for Your wisdom. I've not always taken the time to ask You which way to go before moving forward, or even if I did ask, sometimes I didn't wait patiently for an answer. I desire Your will for my life. I want to be in the right place at the right time. May I move with You, forever listening for Your voice for direction. Show me the way I should go. Speak to me when I've gone off on my own. Bring me back to the place of peace—a place I can only find in You. Your ways are not my ways. Help me to always choose Your path for my life.

· ·

Whether you turn to the right or to the left, your ears will hear a voice behind you, saying, "This is the way; walk in it."
ISAIAH 30:21 NIV

Prospering in the Valley

I've walked through some dark valleys, Father. I know You were there, because I sensed the times You carried me. I don't claim to understand the difficult seasons, Lord. I wish they were fewer and farther between. But there is comfort in knowing that the valleys are easier to navigate now that I understand I'm not alone. You can even show me how to prosper (i.e., do well) during hard seasons. Thank You for never leaving me, and please show me how to be a better friend to those who are walking through valleys today. Amen.

Even when I walk through the darkest valley,
I will not be afraid, for you are close beside me.
Your rod and your staff protect and comfort me.

PSALM 23:4 NLT

New Compassions Every Day

I get it, Lord. I get why You don't want me to go to bed angry. You don't want to let the woes of one day spill over into the next. When I fall asleep in a peaceful state, I can awake to new beginnings. In the same way, I'm grateful that You don't go to bed angry with me when I've had a less-than-stellar day. You love me, forgive me, give me a pat on the back, and promise that Your compassions will be new tomorrow morning. What a faithful God You are. Left to my own devices, I would get stuck in the angst of today. But with You, my future is secure because Your compassions never fail. Thank You, Lord! Amen.

. . . .

Because of the LORD's great love we are not consumed, for his compassions never fail. They are new every morning; great is your faithfulness.

LAMENTATIONS 3:22–23 NIV

Never Give Up

Lord, I don't want to be a quitter; but I've tried so hard to be like You, and I keep messing up. I know You said that with You all things are possible, and I need to be reminded of that daily. Don't let me give up. Help me to remember that You aren't finished with me yet. Amen.

· ·

Wherefore, my beloved, as ye have always obeyed, not as in my presence only, but now much more in my absence, work out your own salvation with fear and trembling. For it is God which worketh in you both to will and to do of his good pleasure.

PHILIPPIANS 2:12–13 KJV

DAY 158

I Declare!

Lord, Your declarations are powerful. But You're teaching me that mine can be powerful too. Today, I openly declare that Jesus Christ is Lord. I choose to believe that You raised Him from the dead, Father. Because I truly believe what I'm declaring, I know that I'm made right with You. What an amazing declaration. It has truly changed my life—and my eternity. All praise to You! Amen.

· ·

If you openly declare that Jesus is Lord and believe in your heart that God raised him from the dead, you will be saved. For it is by believing in your heart that you are made right with God, and it is by openly declaring your faith that you are saved.

Romans 10:9–10 NLT

The Weight of Glory

Oh, how the weight of my troubles can drag me down, Father. Sometimes I feel like I'm down on my knees, crawling along. But I'm grateful today for a different kind of weight—the weight of Your glory. You're developing me, Lord, and forming me into Your image. Thank You for fixing my eyes on the things I cannot see so that I can freely walk toward You. Amen.

. . . .

For our present troubles are small and won't last very long. Yet they produce for us a glory that vastly outweighs them and will last forever! So we don't look at the troubles we can see now; rather, we fix our gaze on things that cannot be seen. For the things we see now will soon be gone, but the things we cannot see will last forever.

2 Corinthians 4:17–18 nlt

DAY 160
Comfort during Loss

Jesus, You know my sorrow, my grief, my pain. No one truly understands my heart—but You. I have a lot of questions I want to know the answers to, and perhaps those answers can only come from You. Show me the path that is right, because sometimes I am blinded by my grief. Hold me tight as I let the tears fall. Wash away the brokenness. Help me let go of the pain and say goodbye to all the hurts. Fill me with Your peace.

Blessed be the God and Father of our Lord Jesus Christ, the Father of mercies and God of all comfort, who comforts us in all our tribulation, that we may be able to comfort those who are in any trouble, with the comfort with which we ourselves are comforted by God.

2 Corinthians 1:3–4 NKJV

Through the Waters

Lord, there have been so many "deep water" situations in my life. Many times, I felt as if I would drown. I nearly lost sight of Your plans for my life. "Tomorrow" felt like an elusive dream. Thank You for the reminder that the things I'm walking through will not consume me. I won't drown, even with the swirling floodwaters threatening to take me down. You have declared this over my life, Father, and I am grateful for Your assurance that I can make it through any situation, good or bad. Amen.

"When you pass through the waters, I will be with you; and when you pass through the rivers, they will not sweep over you. When you walk through the fire, you will not be burned; the flames will not set you ablaze."

ISAIAH 43:2 NIV

You Go Before Me

How secure I felt as a child, Lord, when my mother or father would hold my hand and lead me alongside them. Their long, confident strides gave me courage to trust in where we were headed. The same is true with You. Your strides are long and confident and often stretch far beyond mine, but with Your hand in mine, I feel as secure as I did all those years ago. I'm completely confident that You won't take off running and leave me in the dust. Even when You step out in front of me, You stick close. You care far too much about me to leave me on my own. What a wonderful Father You are! Amen.

"Do not be afraid or discouraged, for the Lord will personally go ahead of you. He will be with you; he will neither fail you nor abandon you."

Deuteronomy 31:8 nlt

Strength to Stand

Lord, as large as my family is, there are bound to be some members whose life views are significantly different from mine. At times, this gets annoying, particularly when they attempt to force their outlook on me. Give me the strength to stand for what I know to be true and help me to love my family despite our differences.

. . . .

In the day when I cried thou answeredst me,
and strengthenedst me with strength in my soul.
PSALM 138:3 KJV

DAY 164

Written on Their Hearts

I get overwhelmed when I think of how personal Your plans for my life are, God. The covenants that You've made with me are, in many ways, like the laws You wrote on the hearts of Your people in Old Testament times. When You take the time to write something on my heart, I know You mean it. You won't go back on Your word. We're talking about a permanent etching here, one that sticks. I'm completely humbled to think You would care enough about me to write something so personal, just for me. Bless You, Father! Amen.

* *

"This is the covenant I will make with the people of Israel after that time," declares the LORD. "I will put my law in their minds and write it on their hearts. I will be their God, and they will be my people."

JEREMIAH 31:33 NIV

Free Indeed

I love the word *truly*, Lord. When You set me free from my past, my addictions, my failures, my woes, my bad attitudes, my habits, my poor relationships, You *truly* set me free. Indeed. How foolish would I be to turn back now, when You've broken chains that held me bound and have released me to new life in You? Oh, Father, You've brought me so far. I don't even like to look back to the way things used to be, except to learn from my mistakes. You've got such an amazing future planned out for me. I wouldn't want to miss a thing. So I'll stand on the outside of those prison walls, forever grateful that You were willing to rescue me, Lord. Truly! Amen.

. . . .

"So if the Son sets you free, you are truly free."
JOHN 8:36 NLT

Oh, Wise One

Sometimes I feel like a little sponge, Lord. I sit there on the counter, dry as a bone, wondering why my life isn't productive. Then I remember why things are going so poorly. I've ceased to spend time with You and in Your Word. So, I race back to Your arms, ready to admit just how much I need You. You brush away every tear and whisper words of great caring into my ears. Only when I spend adequate time with You will I acquire the necessary wisdom to get through the narrow channels in my life, Lord. So today, I choose to remain close. May I be like that little sponge, soaking up all the wisdom I can, both today and in all the days to come. Amen.

. . . .

Get all the advice and instruction you can,
so you will be wise the rest of your life.
PROVERBS 19:20 NLT

Revive My Soul

God, I don't want to miss anything You have for me. I want to know You more. I want to go deeper in my relationship with You. Stir up Your life in me. Give me a desire for revitalization in my soul. Help me recognize distractions that keep me from reaching those goals You want me to reach. Show me how to speak life to others in a way that points them to You. Fill me with a passion for Your kingdom. Speak to me. Guide me. I want to be used for Your glory. May all I do bring You pleasure all the days of my life.

. . . .

Revive us, and we will call upon Your name.
Restore us, O LORD God of hosts; cause Your
face to shine, and we shall be saved!
PSALM 80:18–19 NKJV

Getting Started

Dear Lord, the first step toward any goal is the hardest, and I just don't feel motivated to take it. But there are things I need to do, and so far I haven't found a fairy to do them for me. Procrastination is a terrible hindrance. I know. I'm a closet procrastinator. I don't like to admit to it, but You see it anyway. Thank You for giving me more chances than I deserve. Remind me that I just need to start. Inspiration often springs from soil watered with obedience. Let me learn this lesson well. Amen.

* *

The way of the sluggard is blocked with thorns.
PROVERBS 15:19 NIV

Broken Chains

Wow, what a picture of Your power, Lord! You've broken through gates of bronze and bars of iron to get to me. Even when I was in my deepest, darkest place, You came barreling through, ready to release my chains. And all so that I could have a future. You didn't want to see me bound up, Father, living below my potential. That's the kind of unfailing love You had for me then and have for me even now. You've always wanted to lift me to higher places. Praise You for Your great, inspiring passion for Your children. Amen.

Then they cried to the LORD in their trouble, and he saved them from their distress. He brought them out of darkness, the utter darkness, and broke away their chains. Let them give thanks to the LORD for his unfailing love and his wonderful deeds for mankind, for he breaks down gates of bronze and cuts through bars of iron.

PSALM 107:13–16 NIV

DAY 170
Long Life

I love this promise, Lord! Thank You for this declaration. If I honor my father and mother (and the other elders You've placed in my life), my days will be long. Show me how to respect those You've placed in authority over me. May Your plans for our relationship shine through, even during the tough seasons. And, Father, show me how to lead those You've entrusted to my care (my children or others I teach and tend to). I want them to know the blessing of a good, long life too. May we all, as Your children, learn from You. You're the ultimate Father, and we live to bring honor and glory to Your name. Amen.

• •

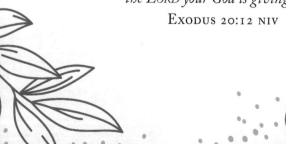

"Honor your father and your mother,
so that you may live long in the land
the LORD your God is giving you."
EXODUS 20:12 NIV

With Gratitude

You have been with me from the beginning, Lord. You have kept my foot from slipping and lifted me out of deep pits. You hold me up when the world falls away before me. You have hidden me from my enemies. You have saved the lives of my family. Forgive me for my complaints. I will never forget Your hand on my life. Thank You for the times You've turned things around and made a way when I could see no way. You have brought me this far, and with gratitude from deep in my heart, I thank You!

. . . .

Then King David went in and sat before the LORD, and he said: "Who am I, Sovereign LORD, and what is my family, that you have brought me this far?"

2 SAMUEL 7:18 NIV

DAY 172

My Work Is a Joy

Lord, You have given me talents and gifts, and I desire to use them for Your glory. Thank You for giving me work to do and for blessing the work of my hands. Help me be diligent in whatever You put before me. May I work earnestly, with honor and integrity. Give me joy as I work because I do everything as unto You. Sometimes work is harder than I expected. Sometimes there are things that seem unfair. Help me remember that You've placed me exactly where You want me. Thank You for the opportunity to touch others with my life. May all I do bring them closer in relationship with You.

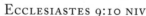

*Whatever your hand finds to do,
do it with all your might.*
ECCLESIASTES 9:10 NIV

All-Knowing

You know, Lord! Even when I don't, You know all things about my journey: which road I should take, which decisions I should make, which plans are established for me. You also know how to speak to my heart and offer guidance every step of the way. You are my all-knowing Father, the only one who truly has my best interest at heart. I settle the issue once and for all, this very day. I trust You to lead me according to Your sovereign will. Amen.

· ·

Oh, the depth of the riches both of the wisdom and knowledge of God! How unsearchable are His judgments and His ways past finding out! "For who has known the mind of the LORD? Or who has become His counselor?"

ROMANS 11:33–34 NKJV

Difficult People

Dear Lord, I ask You to help me be patient and kind today. The Bible speaks about long-suffering. That's what I need as I deal with difficult people and irritating situations. Whether it's squabbling children or rude drivers or harried clerks, I know there will be those today who will irk me. In those moments when I want to scream, help me remember to forbear and forgive. It's just so easy to react, but help me instead to deliberately choose my response. I'm depending on Your power, Father. Amen.

* *

Bear with each other and forgive one another if any of you has a grievance against someone.
COLOSSIANS 3:13 NIV

Your Good Pleasure

The kingdom. Oh, how I love speaking that word. *Kingdom.* Sometimes I feel like a princess in a castle tower, surveying all of the lands below that belong to her father, the king. You are the great and mighty King, Lord, and I'm in awe of Your kingdom—both the earthly kingdom and the heavenly kingdom to come. What truly awes me is that You've chosen to give all of this: the pleasures of a relationship with You here on earth and a heavenly home besides. You must really care a lot about me, Lord. I am Your humble daughter, completely wowed by her Daddy God. Amen.

. . . .

"Do not be afraid, little flock, for your Father has been pleased to give you the kingdom."
LUKE 12:32 NIV

Wherever We Go

I'm remembering my childhood, Lord—how I would climb into the back seat of the car and let my parents take me from place to place. I didn't always know where we were headed, but from the moment I got in that car, I knew I would be safe. The same is true with You, Father. Wherever I go, whether it's to a local supermarket or a mission field halfway across the globe, You're behind the wheel, carrying me safely to where I need to be. What a comfort, to trust in the one who created me to lead me safely on.

"Be strong and courageous. Do not be afraid or terrified because of them, for the LORD your God goes with you; he will never leave you nor forsake you."

DEUTERONOMY 31:6 NIV

His Ways Are Higher

Your ways are higher, Lord. It's not always clear in the moment, but my plans—great as they might seem—don't even come close to Yours, simply because You see what I can't see. You know what I don't know. You care in ways I simply cannot comprehend. When the road You're leading me down makes no sense to my finite mind, Father, sweep in and remind me that Your thoughts, Your ways, are always higher. Amen.

. . . .

"For my thoughts are not your thoughts, neither are your ways my ways," declares the Lord.
Isaiah 55:8 niv

DAY 178
Be Still

I'm so busy, Lord! There are days when I'm rushing here and there and barely pause to catch my breath. On those days, I often forget to meet with You. Sometimes, in the craziness, I also forget that You've already made plans for me. I strike out on my own without asking Your opinion. Thank You for the reminder that pausing to be with You is the first step to a great day. Teach me to be still in Your presence, to wait on You. I'll need a lot of reminding, Lord, but don't give up on me. What a blessing to know that You will fight for me, if I will only slow down long enough to let You. Amen.

* *

"The LORD will fight for you;
you need only to be still."
EXODUS 14:14 NIV

Wise Fear

"The fear of the LORD is the beginning of wisdom" (Psalm 111:10 KJV). Sometimes this passage from Your Word seems almost contradictory, Lord. But there is healthy fear, and then there's crippling fear. I know this passage means that my respect of You is so deep that I abhor sin. Please help me to have this wise fear. Amen.

* *

The fear of the LORD is the beginning of wisdom: and the knowledge of the holy is understanding.
PROVERBS 9:10 KJV

You're Not a Human Being

Your Word is truthful in all situations, Lord. I can trust that what You say will be fulfilled. You're not like the people I've known who say one thing but mean another. Sometimes humans (myself included) have great intentions when they make promises, but they don't follow through. Some say, "Sure, I'll be there for you," and then they're not. But You're not like that, Father. Every promise You've ever spoken (either in Your Word or whispered in my ear) is solid-gold truth. I'm so grateful. Amen.

"God is not human, that he should lie, not a human being, that he should change his mind. Does he speak and then not act? Does he promise and not fulfill?"

NUMBERS 23:19 NIV

Your Words Are Exalted

Lord, Your Word is exalted above all. Even a decree from the greatest ruler on earth can't compare. The opinions of Hollywood stars don't even come close. Even the finest teachers and educators can't speak with the same level of authority that You have. Thank You for the reminder that all I have to do is be still and know that You are God. When I'm in that position of submission, You are exalted in all the earth. Oh, what a magnificent Father You are. Be exalted forever, Lord! Amen.

. . . .

He says, "Be still, and know that I am God;
I will be exalted among the nations,
I will be exalted in the earth."
PSALM 46:10 NIV

Your Great Love

It's the ultimate verse, Lord, the one we hang all of our hopes and dreams on. Your love—that vast, immeasurable, transforming love—offers us new hope. Your plan for us always included a happily ever after with You. What an amazing romancer You are! You woo us to You then provide life eternal. But what a sacrifice You made, sending Your Son so that all of this would be possible. There are no words to express my gratitude, but I will try, Lord. With all of my life, my actions, my thoughts, and my motivations, I will try. Amen.

. . . .

For God so loved the world that he gave his one and only Son, that whoever believes in him shall not perish but have eternal life.

JOHN 3:16 NIV

DAY 183
Unlimited Resources

Father, the Bible says You own "the cattle on a thousand hills." You have unlimited resources. So I'm asking You to supply a special need I have today. Although I try to be a good steward of the money You give me, some unexpected event has caught me without the necessary funds. I know You can remedy this situation, if You deem that good for me. Because You're my Father, I'm asking for Your financial advice. I need Your wisdom in this area of my life. Amen.

*"For every animal of the forest is mine,
and the cattle on a thousand hills."*
PSALM 50:10 NIV

I Live by Faith

It's not about me anymore, Lord. It's all about You. Oh, I know—it used to be about me. Always. My way or the highway. But those days are gone. The old me has vanished. In her place: Jesus Christ, Your Son! This new outlook has taken some getting used to. (I was, after all, looking out for me, myself, and I for a very long time.) But, after all You've done for me, how could I desire any other path? I choose to live by faith in the one who gave Himself for me. May every attitude be a reflection of that decision, Father. Amen.

· ·

I have been crucified with Christ and I no longer live, but Christ lives in me. The life I now live in the body, I live by faith in the Son of God, who loved me and gave himself for me.
GALATIANS 2:20 NIV

To the End of the Age

It's probably a good thing that I don't know how long I'll live, Lord. I don't know the number of my days, but You do. I'm not counting down the minutes, but I am doing my best to live each day with purpose, ready to see Your plans fulfilled in my life. Best of all, I'm enjoying getting to know You more with each passing day. No matter how many years I have left, every one will be spent with Your hand in mine. How remarkable to know that the Creator of the universe cares enough about me to walk with me every day of my life. Praise You for that, Lord. Amen.

· ·

"And surely I am with you always,
to the very end of the age."
MATTHEW 28:20 NIV

You Say I Can Shine Like a Star

I must confess: sometimes my candle feels more like a dying ember than a shining star, Lord. I reach the burned-out stage pretty quickly. Even on the best of days, I don't always shine like I should. Thank You for the reminder that You've called me to shine like the brightness of the firmament. I can only do this if I'm a reflection of You, and that's my chief aim from this moment on. It's not my glory, Father. It's not my light. It's all You, Lord. May I be a beautiful reflection of You. Amen.

. . . .

"Those who are wise will shine like the brightness of the heavens, and those who lead many to righteousness, like the stars for ever and ever."
Daniel 12:3 niv

Until It Is Finally Finished

You're a "never give up" kind of God, and I love that about You. When You start things, You finish them. I wish I could say I had that attribute, but many times I begin projects and give up halfway through. I throw in the towel often before I've even given things a chance. You won't give up on me, Lord, even when I feel like giving up on myself. Whew. That's a comfort. Your work will continue all the way to completion. I don't know what the "completed" me will look like, but You do—and You've already begun the work to get me there. Thanks for hanging in there! Amen.

. . . .

And I am certain that God, who began the good work within you, will continue his work until it is finally finished on the day when Christ Jesus returns.
PHILIPPIANS 1:6 NLT

Lost!

Lord, I've lost my cell phone again! Please help me find it! I know sometimes I'm careless; help me learn from this. But, Lord, You know how much information is in that phone and how much I need it to carry out my responsibilities today. You know where it is right now. Help me think of that place. Guide me to it. And just like the woman with the lost coin—I will rejoice! Amen.

. . . .

"Rejoice with me, for I have found the piece which I lost!"

LUKE 15:9 NKJV

A Face-to-Face Meeting

So many of the situations in my life are muddy, Lord. Unclear. Blurry. Sometimes I wish I had a magic mirror (like the ones in fairy tales) so that I could clearly see what's coming. Thank goodness that You know. And though my vision is imperfect, there's coming a day when everything will make perfect sense. I will see You face-to-face and receive all of the answers to the lingering questions in my life. Until that day, I choose to trust in Your plans, Father, even when they look a bit fuzzy around the edges. Amen.

* *

When I awake, I will see you
face to face and be satisfied.
PSALM 17:15 NLT

Right Paths

Choices, choices. They're everywhere! I could turn to the right. Or the left. I could go forward. Or backward. I could take this job. Or that job. Or even that other job. I could date this person. Or that person. Or the other person. With so many paths in front of me (and so many voices urging me to go this way or that), I could find myself headed in the wrong direction in a hurry. Today, I commit myself to listening carefully to Your voice alone so that I can take the right road. And as I step out onto it, I will receive strength for the journey that only You can give. With every step, I will do my best to bring honor and glory to Your name. Amen.

* *

He renews my strength. He guides me along
right paths, bringing honor to his name.
Psalm 23:3 nlt

You Tell Me to Ask, Seek, Knock

You ask me to take action, Father. You want me to ask, so I come to You boldly, making my request known. You ask me to seek, so, Lord, I seek Your will—and Your way—with my whole heart. Not my will but Yours be done, Father. You ask me to knock, so here I stand, Lord, my knuckles rap-rap-rapping on the door of Your heart. I'm engaged in the process and will hover close, asking, seeking, knocking as long as it takes. I'm so grateful for the open doors You are placing in front of me even now. Amen.

* * *

"So I say to you: Ask and it will be given to you; seek and you will find; knock and the door will be opened to you."

Luke 11:9 niv

Victory!

I love a good victory, Father, whether it's at a ball game, during a volatile political season, or in an argument with an adversary. But there's a greater victory than the ones I see in the temporal realm. When You died on the cross, Jesus, the ultimate victory over sin and death was won. This victory leads to eternal life for all who call on Your name. How can I ever thank You enough for winning that battle on my behalf, Lord? I commit myself enthusiastically to sharing the good news of what You've done so that others can share in this victory too. Amen.

* *

But thank God! He gives us victory over sin and death through our Lord Jesus Christ. So, my dear brothers and sisters, be strong and immovable. Always work enthusiastically for the Lord, for you know that nothing you do for the Lord is ever useless.

1 CORINTHIANS 15:57–58 NLT

Understanding Your Will

So often, I rail against what I do not understand. It's hard to move forward when what's in front of me makes no sense at all. But You're teaching me, Father, that one thing is a given: You have my best interest at heart. So, I choose to keep moving, even when I'm perplexed by the twists and turns in the road. I don't want to be thoughtless. I want every step in my journey to be carefully thought out so that I know without a doubt what You're wanting me to do. If I begin to veer in the wrong direction, please take hold of my hand and lead me back to the right road. May I listen carefully, so that I can understand, Lord. Thank You for Your guidance! Amen.

Show me the right path, O Lord;
point out the road for me to follow.
Psalm 25:4 nlt

A Proper Outlook

So often, Lord, I see relationships crumbling; and much of the time, a money issue is what starts the process. Some people are careless or dishonest in their spending; others just want too much. As a result, there is a lot of bitterness and hatred. Please help me to have a proper outlook when money is involved.

. . . .

He that loveth silver shall not be satisfied with silver; nor he that loveth abundance with increase: this is also vanity.

ECCLESIASTES 5:10 KJV

You See My Steps

Remember that time, Lord, when I missed a step and fell? After I careened downward, I felt the pain of impact. Oh, how it hurt; how I wished I'd seen that stair-step in advance to better navigate my way. You healed my broken body, but You also taught me a life lesson. All of my steps are visible to You. Even in the darkest night as I feel my way along, You see clearly. Move me with confidence toward the future You have planned for me, Father. Even when I can't see where I'm headed, I know that You do. Every step I take is visible, even the bumbling ones. I give You my feet. Be my compass. Be my guide. I will follow where You lead. Amen.

. . . .

"His eyes are on the ways of mortals;
he sees their every step."

Job 34:21 niv

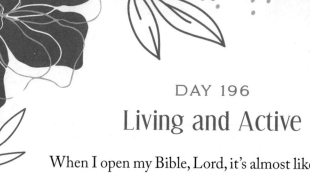

Living and Active

When I open my Bible, Lord, it's almost like the words jump out at me. I can see them as a mighty sword, piercing my heart and cutting to the very place where I need them most. It's an amazing thing, Father, to see how You match the verses with the situations I'm walking through. On those days when I'm feeling a little lost, when I'm not sure where the road is taking me, out springs a verse that gives clear direction. Your Word is alive, Lord! It's breathing. It's active. It's relatable—even in the twenty-first century. How can I ever thank You enough for speaking life to Your children? Praise You for Your Word. Amen.

For the word of God is alive and active. Sharper than any double-edged sword, it penetrates even to dividing soul and spirit, joints and marrow; it judges the thoughts and attitudes of the heart.

HEBREWS 4:12 NIV

You Speak with Authority

All authority. All. What an amazing and bold declaration, Lord! There is no one besides You. No one to ask. No one to approach. No one to beg. You are the be-all and end-all, Father, and Your words (both over my life and over this universe) carry weight. With You, Lord, I can say, "The buck stops here," and mean it. "Whom have I in heaven but you?" (Psalm 73:25 NIV). No one, Father! You are enough. I submit myself to Your holy authority and bend my ear toward heaven, ready to hear Your responses to all of life's questions. Amen.

Then Jesus came to them and said, "All authority in heaven and on earth has been given to me."
MATTHEW 28:18 NIV

Knowing and Known

You've placed so many wonderful people in my life, Lord. I've come to know so many. I've discovered, though, that to be known requires a more intimate relationship. That's what You're asking of me as Your plans are laid out before me: to know and be known. May I know You more as I delve into a deeper relationship with You. As Your plans for my life unfold (and what fun to discover these plans day by day), I feel like I'm getting to know You even more. I'm also getting to know myself, which has been great fun—though a little frightening at times, since I'm so far from perfect. Oh, to know and be known by my Creator! Oh, to walk in intimate relationship with others. What a privilege. Thank You, Father. Amen.

. . . .

"I am the good shepherd; I know my sheep
and my sheep know me."

JOHN 10:14 NIV

God Is a Shield

Protector God, today I'm remembering someone in the armed forces. Though I know war wasn't in Your original plan for this world, it has become a necessary tool for overcoming evil. The Bible recounts stories of You leading Your people, the Israelites, into battle to defend what was right. So there is honor in defending freedom and justice. I ask You to protect this one from danger; dispatch Your peace and put a hedge before, behind, and around him. Watch over all those who are putting their lives in harm's way for my sake. In Christ's name, amen.

. . . .

He shields all who take refuge in him. . . . He trains my hands for battle; my arms can bend a bow of bronze. You make your saving help my shield.
PSALM 18:30, 34–35 NIV

A Strong Support

It's fascinating to think about Your eyesight, Lord. How is it possible to see all of the universe—every planet, every continent, every country, every city, every neighborhood, every home—all at once? I marvel at the very idea. It brings a smile to my face when I think about the fact that You are watching those of us who've committed our lives to You so that You can bring strength. Please look on me today, Father. Give me the strength I need to travel down this road You've placed me on. Thanks for keeping such a good eye on me, Lord. Amen.

. . . .

"For the eyes of the LORD range throughout the earth to strengthen those whose hearts are fully committed to him."

2 CHRONICLES 16:9 NIV

Wisdom and Might

I am created in Your image, Father, and I'm so grateful. I know that wisdom and power are Yours, but I also know that as Your child, I can be wise and powerful too. (One of the perks of being Your child!) Your counsel is the best. I know, because I've applied it to my life on so many occasions. But I'm glad You're teaching me to counsel others as well. May Your understanding and Your wisdom be mine as I walk this road You've laid before me. Have I mentioned how grateful I am that I'm Your daughter, Lord? Amen.

* *

"To God belong wisdom and power;
counsel and understanding are his."

JOB 12:13 NIV

You Say I Can Succeed

The world is full of cheerleaders. I hear them all the time, Lord. They tell me I can get rich quick, that I can lose twenty pounds in a month, that I can lower my interest rate on my credit card and save lots of money. These "cheers" are hyped up and don't ring true. But You, Lord? I love it when You cheer me on! You tell me I can succeed, that I can prosper. You don't offer any get-rich-quick schemes (thank goodness). Instead, You tell me that my success lies in my relationship with You. I'll stick with Your words, Father, that I might experience Your version of success. Amen.

"Keep this Book of the Law always on your lips; meditate on it day and night, so that you may be careful to do everything written in it. Then you will be prosperous and successful."

Joshua 1:8 niv

Carving Channels

Father, what a revelation to know that You go ahead of me and actually carve out channels through the rocks. I would be like a miner lost in the darkened hollows of the shaft if not for You! How remarkable, to think that Your eye sees even the most beautiful gems in the rock You're carving out. Are there diamonds along my path, Father? If so, give me Your vision to see as the road ahead is carved. What a beautiful story You're writing, Lord! I'm so honored You would go to such trouble for me. Amen.

. . . .

"He cuts out channels in the rocks,
and his eye sees every precious thing."
JOB 28:10 NKJV

DAY 204
A Shining Light

Dear God, I want to be a better witness for You. I have friends and family members who don't know You, and every day I interact with people who aren't believers. Lord, I don't want to be corny or pushy, but I do want to let my light shine before others. I ask You to open up the doors for me today. Let me sense Your prompting. And let the silent witness of my life also speak to others about Your great plan of salvation. In Jesus' name, amen.

. . . .

"Let your light so shine before men,
that they may see your good works
and glorify your Father in heaven."
MATTHEW 5:16 NKJV

Broken in the Depths

What an amazing scripture, Lord! By Your knowledge, the oceans, lakes, rivers, streams, and ponds were broken up. Each became its own entity. I know from personal experience that the breaking process isn't always easy, but the outcome is always worth it. Today, I give You permission, as You lay forth the plans for my life, to break me in the depths. Break my heart for what breaks Yours. Break my will so that my selfish desires will fade. Break my pride so that I may be more like You. May I, in the brokenness, become more like You, my Creator. Amen.

. . . .

By wisdom the LORD laid the earth's foundations,
by understanding he set the heavens in place;
by his knowledge the watery depths were
divided, and the clouds let drop the dew.

PROVERBS 3:19–20 NIV

You Are the Potter

You are my potter, Father. You've placed me on the wheel, a formless lump of clay. With Your hands firmly guiding the process, You've shaped me into a visionary, one who sees the vast possibilities for my life. I love what I'm seeing. As You morph me from season to season, I'm growing—spiritually, emotionally, and psychologically. I give You full permission to continue Your work, that Your plan for my life might be all You intended. Thank You, my potter! Amen.

* * *

Woe to those who go to great depths to hide their plans from the LORD, who do their work in darkness and think, "Who sees us? Who will know?" You turn things upside down, as if the potter were thought to be like the clay! Shall what is formed say to the one who formed it, "You did not make me"? Can the pot say to the potter, "You know nothing"?

ISAIAH 29:15–16 NIV

You Make Precious Promises

I love listening when You speak, Lord, especially when You reiterate the promises found in Your Word. Oh, how I love them! You've promised never to leave me or forsake me. You've promised to send the Holy Spirit to comfort me in times of need. You've promised that You will meet all my needs according to Your riches in glory. Through these and hundreds of other promises, I see glimpses of Your divine nature. Thank You that Your promises are true. Amen.

. . . .

And because of his glory and excellence, he has given us great and precious promises. These are the promises that enable you to share his divine nature and escape the world's corruption caused by human desires.

2 Peter 1:4 nlt

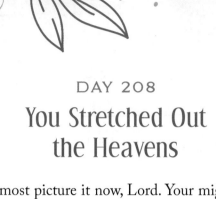

You Stretched Out the Heavens

I can almost picture it now, Lord. Your mighty hand, grabbing hold over the corners of heaven and tugging them into place. You stretched, and things were established. The same has been true in my life, Lord. Your plans have stretched me beyond what I thought I was capable of. Your wisdom has grown me into someone who trusts You more, walks on water with greater assurance, and looks toward the future as a hopeful place. How can I ever thank You enough for growing me into a stronger woman of God? My heart is Yours, Lord. Amen.

"He made the earth by his power; he founded the world by his wisdom and stretched out the heavens by his understanding."

JEREMIAH 51:15 NIV

Called Forth

There's a calling on my life, Lord. I sense it. I feel it. I appreciate it. I choose to respond to it. You've called me with a unique and personalized calling, one that fits like a satin glove. I hear what You're whispering in my ear, that Your intense love for me propelled You to stir my heart to action. Thank You, Father. Knowing that the King of the universe has taken the time to plot, strategize, and implement a plan for my life is amazing. What a blessing! Amen.

. . . .

"Who has done this and carried it through,
calling forth the generations from the
beginning? I, the LORD—with the first
of them and with the last—I am he."
ISAIAH 41:4 NIV

Perfect in Knowledge

Lord, I remember so clearly the times I had to take tests in school, how I prayed for Your divine intervention. I wanted everything I'd learned to root itself in my heart so that I could have a ready answer for every question. How marvelous to realize that You are perfect in knowledge. There's not a test question out there that You can't answer. My mind can't fathom Your ability, Father, but I marvel in the fact that Your ways are perfect. With that in mind, I choose to trust You as I move forward with Your hand in mine. Amen.

. . . .

"Do you know how the clouds hang poised,
those wonders of him who has perfect knowledge?"

JOB 37:16 NIV

Extras

Dear God, I am so thankful that You have provided for me. Sometimes that blessing even goes above and beyond my needs. I now ask for wisdom in handling these gifts. My desire is to glorify You and to make sure that I'm not controlled by money. Please help me use it in a way that honors You. Amen.

. . . .

But my God shall supply all your need according to his riches in glory by Christ Jesus.
PHILIPPIANS 4:19 KJV

You Say I Can Overcome

I don't always feel like an overcomer, Lord. So many times, I just want to crawl into a hole and hide away, to give up completely. But You won't let me! You just keep saying, "You can do this, girl," followed by, "Trust Me" and, "Let Me lead you every step of the way." I'm listening to those words of encouragement today, Father. I really need them. You're an overcomer, and I'm created in Your image, which means I'm an overcomer too. I'll stand in that knowledge today, Lord. Amen.

* *

"I have told you all this so that you may have peace in me. Here on earth you will have many trials and sorrows. But take heart, because I have overcome the world."

JOHN 16:33 NLT

Buoyancy of Faith

God, I've seen swollen rivers; I've watched raging water destroy entire communities. And right now, I feel like the tide of my life is reaching flood level. I'm struggling to keep my head above water, but the waves keep crashing over me. This struggle with depression is almost more than I can bear. Sometimes I just want to surrender to the current and slip under the water. But others are depending on me, and You would be hurt if I chose to end this journey that way. Please hold me up in this flood; Your hands are the only ones that can. Amen.

"When you pass through the waters, I will be with you; and through the rivers, they shall not overflow you."

ISAIAH 43:2 NKJV

Spoken into Existence

Father, I get it! You spoke the world (and everything in it) into existence. Your words brought even the tiniest ladybug to life. Before I was born, You spoke me into existence and knew the paths my life would take. Now, Father, You're teaching me to speak things into existence and to follow the pattern You've set for me. I can look at the situations in my life and speak words of life over them. When I do, the same creative power flows forth. Thank You, Lord, for the ability to speak life. Amen.

*In the beginning God created
the heavens and the earth.*

GENESIS 1:1 NIV

Fullness of Life

I'm so grateful that You're speaking words of life to my heart, Father. There's so much negativity in this world. Sometimes I think the enemy of my soul works overtime to bring me down. But I won't let him. I'll tune out his voice and listen only to what You're saying. What's that? Oh, You want me to know that I have purpose, that my life is going to be rich and full? I'm grateful for the reminder, Lord! Praise You for speaking words of abundant life. Amen.

May you experience the love of Christ,
though it is too great to understand fully.
Then you will be made complete with all the
fullness of life and power that comes from God.
EPHESIANS 3:19 NLT

Keep Me

Dear Father, in the scurry of life, I often forget to be thankful for important things. So many times You've shielded my family from physical harm, and I didn't know it until later. And I'm sure I don't even know about all those moments when You've guarded us from spiritual danger. Although we are the apple of Your eye, I realize we're not immune to trauma and disaster; You won't remove the effects of the curse until the right time comes. But for now, I'm grateful that You care about us and that the only way something can touch us is after it's passed Your gentle inspection. Amen.

* *

Keep me as the apple of the eye,
hide me under the shadow of thy wings.
PSALM 17:8 KJV

You Speak to Me

They are the age-old questions, Lord: How can I hear Your voice? Is it really still and small, or are Your words booming, earthshaking? Can I hear You in the cries of a newborn or in the stillness of a stream trickling over rocks? Will I find Your thoughts in the Bible and carved on my heart? Truth is, I can hear only if my spiritual ears are opened, so today I offer them to You. Speak, Lord, in any way You choose. Bolster my courage. Lift my heart. Whisper, "Attagirl," like only You can. I'm listening, Father. Ears wide open. Amen.

* *

"Have I not commanded you? Be strong and courageous. Do not be afraid; do not be discouraged, for the LORD your God will be with you wherever you go."

JOSHUA 1:9 NIV

Provision for Missions

In Your Word, You've commanded us to take the gospel to all nations. You've also said that when we're obedient, You'll meet our needs. Please meet the needs of our missionaries, Lord. Provide what they need physically and spiritually, and let many souls be saved as a result.

• •

Therefore take no thought, saying, What shall we eat? or, What shall we drink? or, Wherewithal shall we be clothed? . . .for your heavenly Father knoweth that ye have need of all these things.

MATTHEW 6:31–32 KJV

A Godly Example

God, help me to be an example of a faithful disciple of Christ to my family and friends. Those who are close in our lives have the ability to lead us toward or away from righteousness and godliness. I pray that all I do and say will honor You and that I will never be a stumbling block to others. May all within my sphere of influence find me faithful to You. Amen.

. . . .

The righteous is more excellent than his neighbour:
but the way of the wicked seduceth them.
PROVERBS 12:26 KJV

Joy in the Name of the Lord

Father, this morning I meet You here for just a few moments before the busyness of the day takes over. I trust You. It is not always easy to trust, but You have proven trustworthy in my life. I find joy in the knowledge that You are my defender. You go before me this day into battle. I choose joy today because I love the name of the Lord Almighty. Amen.

. . . .

But let all those that put their trust in thee rejoice:
let them ever shout for joy, because thou defendest them:
let them also that love thy name be joyful in thee.

PSALM 5:11 KJV

Role Reversal

Dear Lord, when I was growing up, my parents seemed ageless. But I realize now that my time with them is getting shorter every day. They're getting older, Lord; and, more and more, I find myself looking out for them. This role reversal is really difficult for me. I'm accustomed to them looking out for me, and part of me wishes I could stay in their care for a while longer. Please give me strength to deal with this new phase of our relationship, and help me to honor them as long as they live and beyond. Amen.

* * *

"Even to your old age, I am He, and even to gray hairs I will carry you! I have made, and I will bear; even I will carry, and will deliver you."

ISAIAH 46:4 NKJV

Showing Mercy

Jesus, like the good Samaritan in Your parable, may I too show mercy. Some may never enter the doors of a church, but what a difference an act of grace could make! Put before me opportunities to show unmerited favor. That is, after all, what You have shown to me. You died for my sins. I never could have earned salvation. It is a free gift, an act of grace. Make me merciful. Amen.

. . . .

Which now of these three, thinkest thou, was neighbour unto him that fell among the thieves? And he said, He that shewed mercy on him. Then said Jesus unto him, Go, and do thou likewise.

LUKE 10:36–37 KJV

Anger

God, I need a solution for my anger. Sometimes I let it take over then end up regretting what it leads me to say or do. As I pray and study and grow closer to You, show me ways to control it. Guide me to the right verses to memorize and incorporate into my life. Lead me to someone who can keep me accountable. And, most of all, help me strive for self-control. Amen.

. . . .

If it is possible, as much as depends on you,
live peaceably with all men. Beloved, do not
avenge yourselves, but rather give place to wrath;
for it is written, "Vengeance is Mine,
I will repay," says the Lord.
ROMANS 12:18–19 NKJV

Each One, Chosen

You picked me, Lord! Of all the people in the world (and there are billions), You handpicked me to be a member of the family. It feels so good to be wanted. Needed. Loved. Thank You for arranging Your family across this great big globe as one unit. I have brothers and sisters as far as the eye can see. I need them—and they need me. Together, we are an unstoppable force in You, Lord. Praise You for that. Amen.

. . . .

But in fact God has placed the parts in the body,
every one of them, just as he wanted them to be.
1 CORINTHIANS 12:18 NIV

DAY 225
A God-Centered Home

Father, so many homes are shaken in these days. So many families are shattering to pieces around me. Protect my home, I pray. Protect my loved ones. Be the foundation of my home, strong and solid, consistent and wise. May every decision made here reflect Your principles. May those who visit this home and encounter this family be keenly aware of our uniqueness, because we serve the one true and almighty God. Amen.

* *

Except the Lord build the house, they labour in vain that build it: except the Lord keep the city, the watchman waketh but in vain.

Psalm 127:1 kjv

Natural Consequences

Dear Lord, I know You've forgiven me for that horrible wrong. I thought when I repented that would take care of things, but I'm learning that the natural consequences still hurt. I know they won't disappear, but I pray that You will use them in a positive way—perhaps to keep others from making the same mistake. Amen.

· ·

Blessed is he whose transgression
is forgiven, whose sin is covered.
PSALM 32:1 KJV

Invitation to Rest

Jesus, You told Your disciples to rest. You directed them to leave the crowd and to relax and eat. You saw that they had been busy with ministry and they needed to recuperate. If You directed them to rest, even these twelve who worked at Your side daily, You must want me to rest as well. Remind me to take breaks from ministry. I needed to hear that You give me permission to rest! Amen.

. . . .

*And he said unto them, Come ye yourselves
apart into a desert place, and rest a while:
for there were many coming and going,
and they had no leisure so much as to eat.*
MARK 6:31 KJV

DAY 228
Too Wonderful

So many things seem over my head, Lord. They are above me. When it comes to Your ways, Your Word, Your plans, I guess that's a good thing. If I understood Your ways, if I could comprehend the things You comprehend, then my need for You would be very small, wouldn't it? Oh, but I do need You, Father, and not just because of my lack of understanding. I stand in awe of who You are, Lord, and gaze on Your greatness with awe and wonder. You are too wonderful, Father! Amen.

. . . .

Such knowledge is too wonderful
for me, too lofty for me to attain.
Psalm 139:6 niv

One Step, Two Steps

I haven't counted my steps since I was a child, Lord. I remember doing it, though, to gauge distance. Of course, my tiny strides were a far cry from the steps I take today. It's fascinating to realize that something as small as a step is on Your mind. You have so many other things to keep up with, Father! But there You are, watching me go here and there and keeping track of every step I take. May every move I make bring me closer to You, Lord. I don't want to waste even one step. I want every last one to count and to make a difference for Your kingdom. Use me, Lord, I pray. Amen.

. . . .

"Does he not see my ways and count my every step?"
JOB 31:4 NIV

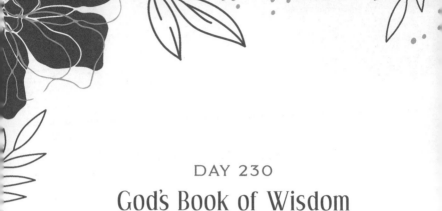

God's Book of Wisdom

There are so many "how-to" books available today, Lord, and they all promise to increase my knowledge in some area. But not one of them gives any hope for added wisdom. Only Your Word offers that. Thank You for providing the means to know You more fully and to live life more abundantly. Amen.

* *

For the word of the Lord is right;
and all his works are done in truth.

PSALM 33:4 KJV

Trust in His Guidance

Father, this morning I come before You and praise You. You are good and loving. You have only my very best interests at heart. Take my hand and lead me. Show me the way to go. Like a child being carried in a loving parent's arms, let me relax and trust You. I know that You will never lead me astray. Thank You, God, for this assurance. Amen.

. . . .

Cause me to hear thy lovingkindness in the morning;
for in thee do I trust: cause me to know the way
wherein I should walk; for I lift up my soul unto thee.
PSALM 143:8 KJV

Spiritual Guardrails

Dear God, help me to erect proper boundaries in my life. I don't want to fall prey to a sin simply because I wasn't being careful. Just like guardrails on a dangerous mountain highway, boundaries in my life keep me closer to center and farther away from the cliffs. I know Satan is plotting my destruction, but Your power is greater. Let me cooperate with Your grace by a careful lifestyle and a discerning spirit. In Christ's name, amen.

. . . .

Stay alert! Watch out for your great enemy, the devil. He prowls around like a roaring lion, looking for someone to devour.

1 PETER 5:8 NLT

Praying for Bold Faith

I desire a bold faith, Jesus. Like the woman who followed You crying out and asking that You cast a demon from her daughter. She was a Gentile, not a Jew; yet, she called You the "Son of David." She acknowledged You as the Messiah. And You stopped. Her faith impressed You. You healed the child. May I be so bold. May I recognize that You are the only solution to every problem. Amen.

. . . .

Then Jesus answered and said unto her, O woman,
great is thy faith: be it unto thee even as thou wilt.
And her daughter was made whole from that very hour.
MATTHEW 15:28 KJV

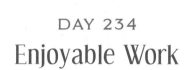

Enjoyable Work

I'm blessed to have a job I enjoy, Lord. So many people aren't able to say the same, and many of them probably have good reason to dislike their work. Thank You for opening this door of opportunity for me. You've met my needs in a wonderful way. Amen.

Not with eyeservice, as menpleasers; but as the servants of Christ, doing the will of God from the heart; with good will doing service, as to the Lord, and not to men.

EPHESIANS 6:6–7 KJV

Twinkle, Twinkle

Lord, You don't just know the number of stars, You actually *determine* the number of stars. You decide where to place them, how big they should be—everything. And You care enough about each one that You take the time to give them names. I'm looking forward to hearing these names when I get to heaven. What fun that will be! You're definitely in the details, Father. Nothing slips by You. To say You care about the little things would be an understatement. If You care about them, I can only imagine how You must feel about us, Your kids. You've called us by name too, and called us to shine just like those stars above. Today, may I shimmer as never before. Thanks for caring so much, Lord. Amen.

* * *

He determines the number of the stars and calls them each by name.

PSALM 147:4 NIV

Come to Jesus

I come to You, Lord Jesus. That is the first step. I come before You now in this quiet moment. As I begin this new day, calm my spirit. There is work that must be done today. But even as I work, I can find rest in You. Ease the tension and stress in me, Lord, as only You can do. Thank You for a sense of peace. Amen.

. . . .

*Come unto me, all ye that labour and are
heavy laden, and I will give you rest.*
MATTHEW 11:28 KJV

Cheerfulness

Jesus, I can't imagine You as a sour, solemn man. I believe You enjoyed life immensely, and I know You brought joy to those around You. Why else would "sinners and tax collectors" want to eat with You (as Your enemies pointed out)? Your mission on this planet was sacred and grave; but I believe Your demeanor in everyday life was buoyant and pleasant. Others loved being in Your presence. Help me pattern my daily attitude after Your example and take heed of Your command to "be of good cheer." Let me reflect You by the way I approach living. Amen.

"Be of good cheer, daughter."
MATTHEW 9:22 NKJV

Following Christ's Example

Lord, You are always there, and You are consistently patient with me. What if it were not so? What if You reached Your limit and showed the wrath that I deserve for my sinful imperfection? Because of Your great patience with me, let me not grow tired of being patient myself. Let me model what You have shown me by Your example. Thank You for Your great patience with me, God. Amen.

* *

And let us not be weary in well doing: for in due season we shall reap, if we faint not.
GALATIANS 6:9 KJV

Prioritizing

Father, I really have a lot to do, and I'm not very good at multitasking. I need Your help each day as I organize the chores that need to be done. Show me how to prioritize my workload so that I can get things done in the most efficient manner, and let my work be pleasing in Your sight. Amen.

* *

But seek ye first the kingdom of God,
and his righteousness; and all these
things shall be added unto you.
MATTHEW 6:33 KJV

The Hairs of My Head

My ability to remember details appears to be waning, Father. Sometimes it's all I can do to remember a friend's birthday or a bill that needs to be paid. The little things slip right by me at times. But You, Lord? You never forget. You're in the details, 100 percent. It boggles my mind to think that You've numbered the hairs of my head. (I lost a few just this morning, Father—but You already knew that!) Even in an ever-changing environment, You still keep track. Oh, to be more like You, Lord. Give me eyes to see (and take care of) the details in my life. Thank You in advance. Amen.

• •

"And even the very hairs of your head are all numbered."
MATTHEW 10:30 NIV

In Christ's Strength

Father, I am so thankful for the strength that is mine as a Christian. I cannot do anything on my own, but through Christ, I can do all things. It is comforting to know that the word *all* includes the trials and concerns that I bring to You this morning. I lay them at Your feet, Lord. I take You at Your Word. I can do all things through Jesus who lives in me. Amen.

* *

I can do all things through
Christ which strengtheneth me.
PHILIPPIANS 4:13 KJV

Blessed Are the Flexible

Flexibility is a struggle for me, God. I don't like interruptions in my routine. It's challenging for me to accept a rerouting of my day. Still, sometimes You have to reorganize for me because I haven't recognized Your promptings. Or maybe there's someone You need me to meet or a disaster You want me to avoid. Help me to accept the detours in my plan today, aware of Your sovereignty over all. Amen.

* *

This is the day the LORD has made;
we will rejoice and be glad in it.
PSALM 118:24 NKJV

Called to Shine

You've called me to shine Your light, Lord. That's an important part of Your plan for my life. Sometimes I feel the pressure of this too keenly. I want to be the best witness for You that I can be. I don't want my light to be a distraction to others; I want it to guide them to You. But I'm so flawed, Father. I make mistakes. Some days I'm like a flickering candle about to burn out. Thank You for giving me multiple chances to shine, Lord. Light the flame once again, I pray. Amen.

"You are the light of the world. A town built on a hill cannot be hidden. Neither do people light a lamp and put it under a bowl. Instead they put it on its stand, and it gives light to everyone in the house. In the same way, let your light shine before others, that they may see your good deeds and glorify your Father in heaven."

Matthew 5:14–16 niv

Your Eyes Saw

It's so fascinating to think that You knew me even before I was born, Lord. Wow! When I was in my mother's womb, You kept careful watch. Even then, You knew who I would become, where I would live, whose lives I would impact. Thank You for calling me even from before my birth, Father! If my mother could trust You with the intimate details of my birth, surely I can trust You with the plans You have for my life. Amen.

. . . .

My frame was not hidden from you when I was made in the secret place, when I was woven together in the depths of the earth. Your eyes saw my unformed body; all the days ordained for me were written in your book before one of them came to be.

PSALM 139:15–16 NIV

DAY 245
Desire Giver

How You love to surprise and delight me, Father! Because You know me so well, You know the little things that will bring a smile to my face. The hidden desires of my heart—the things that even my closest friends and loved ones don't know—are crystal clear to You. And You love to fulfill those desires in ways that only You can. I get a little giddy when I think about how much You love me, Lord. My greatest desire in the world is to know and love You more. Praise You, Father. Amen.

Take delight in the LORD, and he will
give you the desires of your heart.
PSALM 37:4 NIV

Fear No Evil

How wonderful, God, that death has no power over the Christian! You are a strong and mighty God, the one true God. You are with me, protecting me all the way. And when the end of this life comes, whenever that may be, You will walk with me through the valley of the shadow of death. Death has lost its sting because Christ has conquered it! In Your name I pray, amen.

Yea, though I walk through the valley of the shadow of death, I will fear no evil: for thou art with me; thy rod and thy staff they comfort me.

PSALM 23:4 KJV

God's Wisdom

I'm so forgetful! God, I know how many times You've admonished me to seek Your wisdom, yet over and over I try to do things on my own. You'd think I would learn after so many mistakes, but I guess I'm too proud. I don't want to continue like this. I want Your wisdom so that I can live life as You intended. Amen.

. . . .

O the depth of the riches both of the
wisdom and knowledge of God!
ROMANS 11:33 KJV

Lord, Carry My Friend

My friend is hurting, dear Jesus. She's had so many struggles in her life lately, and she feels like she's about to hit rock bottom. I've tried to be there for her, but right now she needs You in a special way. Please let her know that You want to carry her through this trial. Help her to trust You. Amen.

. . . .

A friend loveth at all times.
PROVERBS 17:17 KJV

Starting Where I Am

Jesus, You give tall orders! How can I teach all nations and baptize people? Oh. . .you mean I might not even have to leave my community? There are people all around me who don't know You, Lord. Help me to start with those in my sphere of influence…the grocery store clerk who seems tired and distraught. . .the teacher at my child's school who is so lost. . .Give me the courage to reach out. Amen.

* *

Go ye therefore, and teach all nations,
baptizing them in the name of the Father,
and of the Son, and of the Holy Ghost.
MATTHEW 28:19 KJV

My Source of Strength

Father, at times I worry too much about what others think of me. Even when I just have a minor disagreement with a friend or coworker, I am afraid that the person will not like me anymore. I worry that I have not lived up to what was expected of me. Remind me, Father, that I must seek my ultimate strength and encouragement from You and You alone. Amen.

. . . .

And David was greatly distressed; for the people spake of stoning him, because the soul of all the people was grieved, every man for his sons and for his daughters: but David encouraged himself in the LORD his God.

1 SAMUEL 30:6 KJV

Marked Out for Me

I can see it now, Lord. I'm at the starting block just before a big race. A gunshot splits the air, and I take off, light as a feather. Except this race is my life, and You're the one who has marked it out just for me. A turn to the right, a turn to the left—You've left clear signals at the forks in the road. How grateful I am that You took the time to mark my path. As I aim myself toward You, I will keep my eye on the prize, Father. With a grateful heart, I run. Amen.

. . . .

Therefore, since we are surrounded by such a great cloud of witnesses, let us throw off everything that hinders and the sin that so easily entangles. And let us run with perseverance the race marked out for us.

HEBREWS 12:1 NIV

A Load of Stress

Deadlines, sports schedules, unexpected overnight company—I'm about to pull out my hair! I know we all have our share of stress, but didn't I get an extra load this week, Father? I'm not sure what the purpose of it is, but I know there's a reason. Lord, give me patience through the ordeal, and let me please You. Amen.

. . . .

Take my yoke upon you, and learn of me; for I am meek and lowly in heart: and ye shall find rest unto your souls. For my yoke is easy, and my burden is light.
MATTHEW 11:29–30 KJV

Protection from Temptation

There are temptations all around me, Father. It is easy for me to say no to some of them. But there are subtle ways that Satan tempts me also. The movie that isn't appropriate. . .but all my friends are going to see it. The newest style that is cute and fun. . .but a bit provocative for a Christian woman. Lord, keep my heart focused on You. Protect my heart from the influences of this world. Amen.

* *

Can a man take fire in his bosom,
and his clothes not be burned?
PROVERBS 6:27 KJV

Just Do It

Dear Lord, I want to have an obedient heart. Sometimes, when You speak to me, I feel hesitation or want to postpone what You're telling me to do. Yet that means either I don't trust You or I want my own way, neither of which is good. A child ought to obey her parents because she acknowledges their right to direct her and because she trusts the love behind the words. Help me, Lord, to embrace that kind of attitude when You speak to me. In Christ's name, amen.

* *

But be doers of the word, and not hearers only, deceiving yourselves.
JAMES 1:22 NKJV

A Tailored Witness

Where have You called me to go, Lord? How can I reach others for You? How can I share Your love and Your plan of salvation with those around me? I know You've got specific places and people in mind. You haven't placed me here, where I live and work and play, by accident. You've hand-tailored my surroundings and want me to reach others in my community for You. Show me, Lord. Lead. Guide. Empower. I want to be a witness for You, Father. Amen.

. . . .

"But you will receive power when the Holy Spirit comes on you; and you will be my witnesses in Jerusalem, and in all Judea and Samaria, and to the ends of the earth."

ACTS 1:8 NIV

Serious Warning

Everywhere I look, Father, my society says it's okay. Sex before marriage and outside of marriage. You warn us that this type of sin is of a serious nature. What we do with our bodies stays in our hearts and minds for a very long time. Protect me from the influences in my life that say these things are permissible when Your Word clearly states they are not good for me. Amen.

• •

Flee fornication. Every sin that a man doeth is without the body; but he that committeth fornication sinneth against his own body.

1 CORINTHIANS 6:18 KJV

The Mission Field

Father, I believe the mission field You have for me is right here at home, but I know You want me to be involved in world missions as well. Help me to faithfully pray for our missionaries. Give me wisdom as to how You would have me financially support them, and show me any other way I can help them. Amen.

. . . .

It is more blessed to give than to receive.
ACTS 20:35 KJV

The Simple Life

Dear God, simplicity is a buzzword today. It seems everyone wants "simple" in some fashion. Perhaps it's because life has become too complicated for many of us; we yearn for a more laid-back lifestyle. Lord, I need to simplify my goals in my relationships and my work. Doing so will help me to have a more laser-like focus. And in my spiritual life, a little simplifying might be good too. Instead of trying to conquer large portions of scripture daily, help me to focus on a few verses, thus letting myself steadily grow in understanding. Lord, help me keep simple goals and a simple faith as I simply live for You. Amen.

. . . .

Aspire to lead a quiet life, to mind your own business,
and to work with your own hands.

1 Thessalonians 4:11 NKJV

Straightened Paths

Okay, I'll admit it, Lord. When I make plans, they zigzag all over the place. Oh, initially they don't. I start off on the straight and narrow, but as I go along, things get a little crazy. Before I know it, what looked like a step forward becomes a jog to the right. And what looked like a simple step toward a goal becomes a complicated, dizzying journey I'm completely unprepared for. I'm so excited about the fact that You're a path straightener. Whew! You take my zigzags and turn them into a sensible road, one I can easily navigate with Your help. Thank You, Father. Amen.

* *

Trust in the Lord with all your heart and lean not on your own understanding; in all your ways submit to him, and he will make your paths straight.
PROVERBS 3:5–6 NIV

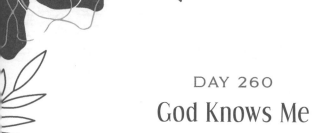

God Knows Me

God, the Bible says that You knew me even before I was formed in my mother's womb. I find confidence in this. You have been with me all along this journey! As I face this day, help me to remember that I am never alone. You go before me to prepare the future. You walk with me through the present. And You were there with me since before I was born. Wow! Amen.

. . . .

*For thou hast possessed my reins: thou hast covered
me in my mother's womb. I will praise thee; for I
am fearfully and wonderfully made: marvellous are
thy works; and that my soul knoweth right well.*

PSALM 139:13–14 KJV

Martha's Trap

Lord, I want to be a servant, but I want it to be done Your way. Please don't let me get caught in Martha's trap of meeting only the physical needs. Although those elements are important, they don't reach the whole person. Let me be a blessing in the spiritual and emotional areas too. Amen.

· ·

*Give, and it shall be given unto you; good
measure, pressed down, and shaken together,
and running over, shall men give into your
bosom. For with the same measure that ye mete
withal it shall be measured to you again.*
LUKE 6:38 KJV

God Hears My Prayers

Lord, the gods of other religions are not approachable. Their subjects bow before them in anguish, hoping to find favor in their sight. These gods are not real. You are the one true and living God, a loving heavenly Father. I love that Your Word says I can come before You with confidence. You hear my prayers. You know my heart. Thank You, Father. Speak to my heart as I meditate upon Your Word now. Amen.

. . . .

And this is the confidence that we have in him,
that, if we ask any thing according
to his will, he heareth us.

1 John 5:14 KJV

Reached Goals

Sometimes I get a little discouraged, Jesus. I feel like I've reached all the goals I've set for myself and that there's nothing for me to achieve that would bring any excitement. Please give me a new outlook. Give me wisdom as I set new goals, and help me to give You the glory when I succeed. Amen.

. . . .

*For wisdom is better than rubies; and all the things
that may be desired are not to be compared to it.*
PROVERBS 8:11 KJV

To Prepare a Place

It boggles my mind to think about heaven, Lord. And yet, You're already there, preparing a place for me. Your plans for me don't just include the here and now but the hereafter as well. This life of mine is well thought out, isn't it? You haven't left anything to chance. You've breathed new life into my spirit so that I can walk out Your plan here on earth and settle into my mansion in heaven once this life is through. What an amazing and generous Father You are! Amen.

"My Father's house has many rooms; if that were not so, would I have told you that I am going there to prepare a place for you? And if I go and prepare a place for you, I will come back and take you to be with me that you also may be where I am."

JOHN 14:2–3 NIV

When to Remain Silent

Heavenly Father, Your Word says that the tongue has great power. My words can help or harm. There are times when silence is best. Help me to know the difference between times I should speak and times I should keep still. I pray for wisdom as I go through this day. I want my speech to honor You. Put a guard over my lips, I pray. Amen.

. . . .

In the multitude of words there wanteth not sin: but he that refraineth his lips is wise.
PROVERBS 10:19 KJV

Still Working on Me

Dear God, I'm a far cry from perfect, but I'm confident in the knowledge that You love me just as I am. You are the one who has begun a work in me, and You will be faithful to complete what has been started. What a thrill to know that You'll make me what You want me to be. Amen.

· ·

Let not mercy and truth forsake thee:
bind them about thy neck; write them
upon the table of thine heart.

PROVERBS 3:3 KJV

Meekness

Heavenly Father, I want to develop the characteristic of meekness, a kind of quiet strength. Rather than a sign of a pushover, meekness is a trait of the strong. It takes guts to be silent when you want to speak. Meekness is not a goal for the weak of heart. It is, rather, for those who would be in the forefront of spiritual growth. Like Moses, the meekest man on earth (see Numbers 12:3), we can reap the rewards of quiet strength in our lives. Amen.

. . . .

With all lowliness and meekness, with longsuffering,
forbearing one another in love.
EPHESIANS 4:2 KJV

Strengthened with Power

It's a glorious feeling, Father, to wake up feeling so refreshed and so energized that I could take the world by storm. That's what it's like after spending time in Your presence too. When I take the time to bring my needs and my concerns to You, I leave feeling much better. You pour out Your Spirit, and that amazing supernatural energy of Yours empowers me. I can't drum up this kind of power, Father. It comes only from You. I'm so very grateful for Your strength, Lord! Amen.

For this reason I kneel before the Father, from whom every family in heaven and on earth derives its name. I pray that out of his glorious riches he may strengthen you with power through his Spirit in your inner being.
EPHESIANS 3:14–16 NIV

Applying Instruction

God, give me ears to hear. Sharpen my senses and make me wise. I am often proud. I think I know it all. But I don't. I need instruction from You. I know this comes in many forms: through reading and meditating on Your Word, through Your people, and through circumstances. Help me to be a good listener and to apply the instruction You send my way. I want to be wise, Father. Amen.

. . . .

Hear counsel, and receive instruction,
that thou mayest be wise in thy latter end.
PROVERBS 19:20 KJV

Right Paths

The right path is often the one less traveled. I am learning this, Father, oh so slowly. You will always lead me in the right path. You will never lead me astray. I have been at the crossroads many times, and I will face such choices again and again. Keep my heart focused on You so that I might be led down pleasant paths, paths that will glorify my King. Amen.

· ·

I have taught thee in the way of wisdom;
I have led thee in right paths.
PROVERBS 4:11 KJV

Balancing Work and Rest

I had to chuckle as I read the verse that says, "Give not sleep to thine eyes" (Proverbs 6:4 KJV). I guess I don't have much trouble obeying that! I have more difficulty with "Come. . .apart. . .and rest a while" (Mark 6:31 KJV). I think I'm getting the picture, though. Please help me learn to balance work and rest. Amen.

. . . .

My presence shall go with thee,
and I will give thee rest.
EXODUS 33:14 KJV

Legacy

Dear God, what kind of legacy am I leaving? I want to be remembered as more than a woman who dressed nicely, had a great family, and went to church. I want to be remembered for the way I invested myself in the lives of others. After all, love is the only lasting thing on this earth, something that will remain when I am physically gone but living with You in eternity. Lord, let my legacy be wrapped up in serving others in love. In Jesus' name, amen.

Prophecy and speaking in unknown languages and special knowledge will become useless. But love will last forever!

1 Corinthians 13:8 nlt

A Way of Escape

I feel like I'm trapped in a dark alley at times, Lord, with no escape route. My own actions—well intentioned as they might be at times—take me to places that leave me feeling stuck. Oh, but how wonderful Your plans are! You always provide a way of escape for me, even when I've painted myself into a corner. Thank You for coming to my rescue, Father. I can't promise it won't happen again, but I do promise to resist temptation with Your help. Amen.

* *

The Lord knoweth how to deliver the godly
out of temptations, and to reserve the unjust
unto the day of judgment to be punished.
2 Peter 2:9 kjv

DAY 274

Generosity

Father, the psalmist declares that he has never seen the righteous forsaken or his children going hungry. This inspires me. I know that You bless those who give. I want to leave a legacy of generosity for my children or for others who are influenced by my life. What they see me practicing regarding giving will impact their choices. May we be a generous family, always looking for opportunities to show mercy. Amen.

. . . .

*I have been young, and now am old; yet have
I not seen the righteous forsaken, nor his
seed begging bread. He is ever merciful,
and lendeth; and his seed is blessed.*

PSALM 37:25–26 KJV

A Woman Who Fears the Lord

God, I want to be a Proverbs 31 woman. My focus should not be on external beauty or the clothing and jewelry that I wear. Rather, may others notice my heart that is forever seeking You. I want nothing more than to be known as a woman of God. Protect me from vanity. Outward beauty is not lasting, but a beautiful spirit is. I meditate upon Your Word now, Lord. I want to honor You. Amen.

Favour is deceitful, and beauty is vain:
but a woman that feareth the LORD,
she shall be praised.
PROVERBS 31:30 KJV

Hospitality

Dear Lord, I need to improve my skills in hospitality. Because You have blessed me, I need to share with others. In fact, hospitality is one of those virtues the apostle Paul commanded of the church. Sharing my home with others is my Christian duty and also a great way to reach out to unbelievers whom I have befriended. Please let me not dread hosting others but rather find ways to make it doable and enjoyable for all. In Jesus' name, amen.

* *

Use hospitality one to another without grudging.
1 PETER 4:9 KJV

That Your Joy May Be Full

It gives me great joy to plan things, Lord. Christmas dinner, parties, family gatherings—I love putting those plans together. And I do it all with others in mind. I can envision the looks on their faces as they partake of the foods I've made, the packages I've wrapped. What joy it must bring You to create plans for my life. Thank You for allowing that joy to spill over as I walk out the path You have laid for me. You've done it all with me in mind, and I'm forever grateful. Praise You, Father! Amen.

. . . .

"I have told you this so that my joy may be in you and that your joy may be complete."

JOHN 15:11 NIV

Christlikeness

There's such a fine line between self-esteem and arrogance. Sometimes I have trouble distinguishing between the two. Father, You created me in Your image. For that I am thankful, but I need to remember that I'm not perfect. Help me not to be proud but to daily strive to be more like You. Amen.

. . . .

When pride cometh, then cometh shame:
but with the lowly is wisdom.
PROVERBS 11:2 KJV

A Friendlier World

Dear God, I was just noticing all the people around me who really could use a friend. For whatever reason, they're alone and hurting. I need to reach out to them. I ask You to give me opportunities and ideas to let them know I care. Let me make the world a little friendlier for them. Amen.

· ·

Finally, be ye all of one mind, having compassion one of another, love as brethren, be pitiful, be courteous.
1 PETER 3:8 KJV

Consulting Christ

Lord, often in my daily planning I forget to consult You. Then I wonder why things don't work out the way I think they should. Forgive my arrogant attitude. I know that only as You guide me through the day will I find joy in accomplishments. Show me how to align my goals with Your will. Amen.

. . . .

Trust in the Lord with all thine heart;
and lean not unto thine own understanding.

PROVERBS 3:5 KJV

Tithing

Father, You tell me to test You with my tithe. If I give it generously, You will bless my household. I will find it overflowing with blessing. There will not be enough room to contain all of it. I imagine the windows of heaven opening and blessing just pouring, pouring, pouring down on me! You are not a God who sprinkles blessings or gives them in little pinches or samples. You are an extravagant giver. Amen.

* *

Bring ye all the tithes into the storehouse. . .
and prove me now herewith, saith the LORD
of hosts, if I will not open you the windows
of heaven, and pour you out a blessing.
MALACHI 3:10 KJV

A Testimony

My life is a song of praise to You, my faithful Father, the giver of life! When people hear my testimony of Your goodness, may they come to know You. I want others to notice the difference in me and wonder why I have such joy, such peace. May I point them to You, Lord, and may they trust in You for salvation. You are the way, the truth, and the life. Amen.

. . . .

And he hath put a new song in my mouth,
even praise unto our God: many shall see it,
and fear, and shall trust in the LORD.

PSALM 40:3 KJV

The Teacher of All Things

My ability to retain the things I learned in school is limited at best. And, while I'd like to consider myself to be a good student, Lord, I often fall short—even when You're trying to teach me a life lesson. Thank You for sending Your helper, the Holy Spirit. What a blessing, to know that Your plans for my life will all become clearer with His help. You are the teacher of all things, Father, which means that You have high hopes for me! I'm so grateful, Lord. Amen.

* *

"But the Advocate, the Holy Spirit, whom the Father will send in my name, will teach you all things and will remind you of everything I have said to you."
JOHN 14:26 NIV

DAY 284

Blessing Those Who Hurt You

God, when someone hurts me, I don't feel like blessing him or her. Remind me what Your Word teaches about love. Love keeps no record of wrongs. Love forgives. It restores. Love tries again. Love lets it go. Love blesses even when it's not my turn to bless! Give me a spirit of love that trumps evil. And allow me to bless those who hurt me. I can only do so in Your power. Amen.

. . . .

Not rendering evil for evil, or railing for railing:
but contrariwise blessing; knowing that ye are
thereunto called, that ye should inherit a blessing.
1 PETER 3:9 KJV

Sensory Joys

Dear God, thank You for the five senses—sight, sound, touch, smell, and taste. You could have designed a virtual world, but instead You created one that can be experienced. Today, I want to revel in the fact that I'm alive. I want to delight in the tactile joys I often take for granted. I'm grateful for each one. Amen.

. . . .

For in him we live, and move, and have our being.
ACTS 17:28 KJV

DAY 286
In Harm's Way

Dear God, so many missionaries are in harm's way. They face terrorist threats, unsanitary living conditions, and even dangerous animals or illnesses that I can't begin to fathom. Please protect them, Father. They've willingly taken these risks so that others might know Your love. Keep them under Your wing of safety. Amen.

. . . .

Unto the upright there ariseth light in the darkness:
he is gracious, and full of compassion, and righteous.
PSALM 112:4 KJV

A Thankful Heart

Lord, everything good in my life comes from You. Often, I forget to thank You. I am thankful for Your provision and Your protection. I am thankful for my family and friends. I am most of all thankful for the joy of my salvation, which comes through Christ. Give me a grateful heart, I pray. Let me always remember that every good and perfect gift comes from Your hand. Amen.

· ·

And let the peace of God rule in your hearts,
to the which also ye are called in one
body; and be ye thankful.
COLOSSIANS 3:15 KJV

Acquainted with All My Ways

I often use the phrase "No one knows me like I know myself," but that's not true, Lord. You know me better than I know myself. You know every detail—my likes, my dislikes, my hopes, my dreams, my disappointments, my joys. You're acquainted not only with the things I've done in the past but also with what I hope to accomplish in the future. Because You know me from the inside out, I am confident in Your ability to scrutinize my path and make a way for me. It's exciting to see where You will take me next, Lord. Amen.

* * *

You know when I sit and when I rise; you perceive my thoughts from afar. You discern my going out and my lying down; you are familiar with all my ways.

Psalm 139:2–3 niv

All of Me

When You were asked what the greatest commandment was, You did not evade the question. You answered clearly, Jesus. I am to love the Lord my God with all of my heart, soul, mind, and strength. I am to love my God with all of me. There should be nothing left over when I am finished loving God. No crumbs I feed to the idols that crave my attention. It is all for You. Amen.

. . . .

And thou shalt love the Lord thy God
with all thy heart, and with all thy soul,
and with all thy mind, and with all thy
strength: this is the first commandment.
MARK 12:30 KJV

DAY 290

Special to the Father

How can I doubt my worth in Your eyes, Father? You know the number of hairs on my head. You created me, and You said that Your creation is very good. When I'm tempted to get down on myself, remind me that I am special to You and that there's no one just like me. Amen.

. . . .

In the multitude of my thoughts within me thy comforts delight my soul.
PSALM 94:19 KJV

The Real Me

Heavenly Father, so many people in my world wear masks. We earth dwellers are afraid to be real with others; we fear losing the respect and esteem of our peers. And, oddly enough, we're often afraid to be real with even You—and You know everything about us anyway. I want to be genuine in my approach and interaction with others, including You. Give me the courage to reject the lure of artificial "perfectness" and, instead, live out my life and relationships in a real way. Amen.

. . . .

I have chosen the way of truth.
PSALM 119:30 NKJV

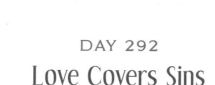

Love Covers Sins

Lord, all of my sin was nailed to the cross when Your Son died for me. Without grace, I am but filthy rags before a holy God. But through Christ, I am adopted as Your daughter, forgiven. There is pride in this daughter, God. Pride that resists forgiveness. Pride that says "I am right." Remind me of the multitude of my own sins that Your love covered through Jesus. Help me to love others well. Amen.

. . . .

Hatred stirreth up strifes: but love covereth all sins.
PROVERBS 10:12 KJV

Finding Time to Rest

I find it difficult to even sit down to a meal, Father. Resting seems like such a far-fetched notion. I know You want me to find time to rest and spend time with You, but I'm on the go constantly, and I still don't get everything done. Please help me, Lord, to make resting a priority. Amen.

* * *

*Cast thy burden upon the L*ORD*, and he shall sustain thee: he shall never suffer the righteous to be moved.*
PSALM 55:22 KJV

Fixed by His Authority

We are ruled by the clock, Lord. It tells us when to wake up, when to go to work, when to eat, when to sleep. The hours and minutes are fixed. Set. Always the same, day after day. Your times are fixed too, Lord. When You set a plan in motion, it has a timeline. And though I can't see this timeline, I can trust in the fact that it was set in place by Your authority. I can trust Your timetable, Father. I choose to trust, even when it appears to throw me off course. Amen.

· ·

He said to them: "It is not for you to know the times
or dates the Father has set by his own authority."
ACTS 1:7 NIV

Showing That I Love God

How do I show that I love You, God? It must be more than merely a phrase I use in prayer. The way I show it is to keep Your commandments. I need Your strength for this. I fail every day. Renew my desire to live according to Your principles. They are not suggestions. They are commands. Honoring them will cause me to see You at work in my life. I love You, Lord. Amen.

* *

He that hath my commandments, and keepeth them, he it is that loveth me: and he that loveth me shall be loved of my Father, and I will love him, and will manifest myself to him.

JOHN 14:21 KJV

Time Management

Dear God, sometimes I think I need more than twenty-four hours in my day! It seems I never have enough time. I think with longing about simpler seasons in my life when I could actually complete my to-do lists. There was such satisfaction in having a few stress-free moments. Now, my schedule is filled, and I'm so harried. Holy Spirit, please guide in this area of my life. How I use my time is part of stewardship, so I'm asking for Your wisdom. Show me how to manage the hours I have so I can honor You in everything I do. In Christ's name, amen.

. . . .

Teach us to number our days,
that we may gain a heart of wisdom.
PSALM 90:12 NIV

Amazing Grace

Lord, I get so caught up in trying to do good works sometimes. I need to remember that I am saved by grace. You are pleased with me simply because I believe in Your Son, Jesus, and have accepted Him as my Savior. You do not bless me or withhold good gifts based on my performance. Remind me of Your amazing grace, and make me gracious with others. In Jesus' name I pray, amen.

* *

For by grace are ye saved through faith; and that not of yourselves: it is the gift of God: not of works, lest any man should boast.
EPHESIANS 2:8–9 KJV

Harmful Relationships

Lord, I generally think of relationships as being between people, and I fail to remember that my relationship to things can seriously affect how I react to people. For instance, sometimes I get so involved in a television show that I fail to give needed attention to my family. Forgive me, Father. Be in charge of my relationships. Amen.

. . . .

And beside this, giving all diligence, add to your faith virtue; and to virtue knowledge; and to knowledge temperance; and to temperance patience; and to patience godliness; and to godliness brotherly kindness; and to brotherly kindness charity.

2 PETER 1:5–7 KJV

Perseverance

Lord, I so often reach the point of giving up when I'm following my own path. Somehow, knowing You're the one with the plan gives me the wherewithal to keep going. I'll persevere, Father, because I know You're ultimately the one in charge. I submit myself to Your will and Your process, Lord. It's not always easy, but I will do my best to put one foot in front of the other as I walk out this remarkable plan You've set in motion for my life. Amen.

. . . .

You need to persevere so that when you have done the will of God, you will receive what he has promised.

HEBREWS 10:36 NIV

Steward of Grace

Thank You for the gifts You have given me, Lord. I look around at the other believers in my life. We are all gifted in different ways. Help me to be a good steward of the gifts You have entrusted me with in this life. Instead of looking out for myself, may I have opportunities to use my abilities to minister to others. I understand that it is in doing so that I honor You. Amen.

As every man hath received the gift,
even so minister the same one to another,
as good stewards of the manifold grace of God.
1 PETER 4:10 KJV

DAY 301

The Power of Words

Father, my mouth sometimes gets me into trouble. Please keep me aware of the things I say that aren't right. Let me back up and apologize if I've hurt anyone. Better yet, let me consider my words before I cast them out on the wind. Once spoken, they can never be recalled. Your written Word is living, brilliant, and powerful; Jesus is the embodiment of it—the Living Word. My spoken earthly words are weighty as well; they can minister life or death to those who hear. I ask You to remind me of this throughout the day. Amen.

* *

Death and life are in the power of the tongue:
and they that love it shall eat the fruit thereof.
PROVERBS 18:21 KJV

An Heir to the King

Heavenly Father, thank You for adopting me as an heir to the King of kings! You provided a way for me to come before You, holy God. Christ carried my sin as His burden. It was nailed to the cross and has been forgiven forever, once and for all. Thank You for the abundant life that is mine because I am Yours. I praise You for viewing me through a lens called grace. Amen.

. . . .

That being justified by his grace, we should be made heirs according to the hope of eternal life.
TITUS 3:7 KJV

Hope for the Future

Lord, I can't see the future. I see only one piece of the puzzle at a time, but You see the finished product. As I go through this day, I will not fear because You are in control. When things seem hopeless, there is hope. My hope is in a sovereign God who says He knows the plans He has for me. I am counting on You to see me through. Amen.

. . . .

For I know the thoughts that I think toward
you, saith the LORD, thoughts of peace, and
not of evil, to give you an expected end.
JEREMIAH 29:11 KJV

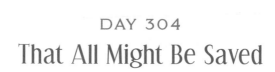

DAY 304

That All Might Be Saved

Of all the plans You've set in motion, Lord, this one's my favorite. It is Your good and perfect will that all will be saved. All—everyone! People across this beautiful planet are all loved by You (even people who are radically different from me). Thank You for including me in the plan to reach people with the gospel, Father. May I be an example of all Your love, Your grace, Your peace. And while I'm waiting for those around me to come to a knowledge of the truth, may I exemplify Your gracious heart toward them. Amen.

· ·

This is good, and pleases God our Savior,
who wants all people to be saved and to
come to a knowledge of the truth.
1 TIMOTHY 2:3–4 NIV

Loving My Enemies

Lord, some of Your commands are easy to understand, such as taking care of widows and orphans. But some of them go against human nature. It's easier to show mercy to those we love, but You tell us to love our enemies. You command us to love those who are hard to love. Give me a love for the unlovable, Father. I want to have a heart that pleases You. Amen.

. . . .

For if ye love them which love you, what reward have ye? do not even the publicans the same? And if ye salute your brethren only, what do ye more than others? do not even the publicans so?
MATTHEW 5:46–47 KJV

Gossip

Lord, I got caught in gossip today. I didn't mean to, though. A group of us were just talking about this and that, and You know how women are. We're so into relationships and what others are doing. Before long, the conversation had dug itself a little too deep into someone else's life. I tried to stop listening but didn't try hard enough. By the time we broke up our little gabfest, I felt terribly guilty. Please forgive me, Father. Give me the courage to make the right decision next time; help me refuse to listen to negative stories about someone who is not there to defend themselves. In Jesus' name, amen.

* *

Let all. . .evil speaking be put away from you, with all malice.
EPHESIANS 4:31 NKJV

Not in Myself

The world tells me to look within, Lord. I'm told that everything I need to know about myself, for myself, is already inside me. Oh, Father, what a foolish notion! The answers aren't found in me. I can plan and devise all I like, but the only true answers are found in You. If I set my own course, I'm sure to land in a ditch. You direct my path. You make the plans. I'll do my best to lean close and listen as You lead me along a better path. Amen.

. . . .

LORD, I know that people's lives are not their own; it is not for them to direct their steps.

JEREMIAH 10:23 NIV

All I Need

Heavenly Father, You are a God of hope, joy, and great love. I don't need signs or wonders. I often wait for people or situations to turn from hopeless to hopeful. But my hope is in You. I need not wait for anything else or look for some other source. I quiet myself before You this morning and ask that You renew the hope within my heart. Thank You, Father. Amen.

* *

And now, Lord, what wait I for?
my hope is in thee.
PSALM 39:7 KJV

Engraved on Your Palms

Lord, You care so deeply for me. I am in wonder and awe as I think about the fact that Your plans for my life are engraved on Your hands. Oh, those wonderful, perfect hands! They lead me, they guide me, they lift me up when I fall. And what an amazing thought, to know that You care enough about me to carry a permanent marking of love. How can I praise You for caring so deeply for me, Father? I stand amazed. Amen.

* * *

"See, I have engraved you on the palms of my hands; your walls are ever before me."
ISAIAH 49:16 NIV

The Best Relationship

Dear Jesus, I've known many people in my life. I've enjoyed many good relationships and tried to avoid the bad. One thing is certain, though. My relationship with You is the most important. I'm so glad You have time for me and that You want me to fellowship with You. I couldn't ask for a better friend. Amen.

. . . .

The LORD thy God in the midst of thee is mighty; he will save, he will rejoice over thee with joy; he will rest in his love, he will joy over thee with singing.

ZEPHANIAH 3:17 KJV

Fixing My Thoughts

God, today I'm having a pity party. My thoughts are so focused on earthly things that I am having trouble looking up. I could mope around here all day, but I guess it's time for the music to stop and the party to end. Lord, You can't work through me when I'm feeling sorry for myself. Forgive me for my pettiness, and let me respond to life with maturity. Help me to focus on good, praiseworthy things. In Christ's name, amen.

* * *

Fix your thoughts on what is true, and honorable, and right, and pure, and lovely, and admirable.
PHILIPPIANS 4:8 NLT

DAY 312

Love in Deed and Truth

Father, it is easy to say the words "I love you," but it is harder to live them. You want Your children to love their enemies. You tell us to love through action and with truth. These are high callings that require Your Holy Spirit working in us. Use me as a vessel of love today in my little corner of the world. Let me love through my deeds and not just with words. Amen.

* *

My little children, let us not love in word,
neither in tongue; but in deed and in truth.

1 JOHN 3:18 KJV

Bless His Name

Jesus, You alone are worthy of all of my praise. I bless Your name. One day, I will worship You with no end, no holding back, and no earthly distraction. I will worship You in heaven forever and ever. . .with the angels and with all of Your people. For today, I go into Your world, and I will choose to bless Your name in the present. Accept my offering of praise. Amen.

. . . .

And I beheld, and I heard the voice of many angels round about the throne and the beasts and the elders: and the number of them was ten thousand times ten thousand, and thousands of thousands; saying with a loud voice, Worthy is the Lamb that was slain to receive power, and riches, and wisdom, and strength, and honour, and glory, and blessing.
REVELATION 5:11–12 KJV

Do Not Fear

Maybe it's just my controlling nature, Father, but I have a hard time not being afraid. You ask me to take my hands off, to let You be in charge. The idea of letting go of the reins is frightening. But today, I choose to let go of fear as I release my hold on the reins of my life. (They were never mine to hold in the first place, were they?) And while trusting Your plans for my life is hard, I know You will grow my faith with each step I take. I also know You're working for my good, Lord. Thank You for that. Amen.

"So do not fear, for I am with you; do not be dismayed, for I am your God. I will strengthen you and help you; I will uphold you with my righteous right hand."

ISAIAH 41:10 NIV

The Beauty of the Lord

May my pursuit of You, Lord, be my "one thing." May I praise You and serve You in this life, which is but training camp for eternity! I look forward to heaven, Father, where I may truly know the depths of Your beauty. I see glimpses of Your beauty in Your creation. One day, it will be fully revealed. What a glorious day that will be! Until then, be my "one thing." I love You, Lord. Amen.

. . . .

One thing have I desired of the LORD, that will I seek after; that I may dwell in the house of the LORD all the days of my life, to behold the beauty of the LORD, and to enquire in his temple.

PSALM 27:4 KJV

Music

Dear Lord, music is the universal language of the human family. Today, music is available on a multitude of electronic devices. And there are so many genres—an array of listening options. Some appeal to me; others don't. But I want to base my choices on Your principles. What I listen to will affect my mood, my attitude, and my spiritual state of being. Holy Spirit, give me discernment. Let the music to which I listen not go counter to what You're trying to do in me. Amen.

. . . .

Whatsoever ye do, do all to the glory of God.
1 CORINTHIANS 10:31 KJV

Only One Master

Father, there are so many things in this world that fight for my affection. It seems there is always a new product or style that the advertisements say I can't live without! It is easy to get caught up in materialism. Guard my heart, Father, and guard even my tongue. Remind me that the word *love* should not be used loosely. I love You, Father. Be Lord of my life, I pray. Amen.

. . . .

No man can serve two masters: for either he
will hate the one, and love the other; or else
he will hold to the one, and despise the other.
Ye cannot serve God and mammon.
MATTHEW 6:24 KJV

Modest Example

So many people think that modesty is only a clothing issue, but You've shown me that it's so much more. It's an attitude akin to humility, and it's what You want from me. Even in this You set the example for me, Jesus. Help me to follow the pattern You've given me. Amen.

. . . .

In like manner also, that women adorn themselves in modest apparel, with shamefacedness and sobriety; not with broided hair, or gold, or pearls, or costly array; but (which becometh women professing godliness) with good works.
1 TIMOTHY 2:9–10 KJV

Revealed through the Spirit

Sometimes I forget, Lord. I forget that revelation only comes through You. I want to obtain answers—direction—in the usual ways: from friends, loved ones, acquaintances. Even from my own knowledge, obtained from years of walking this planet. Advice is good. Knowledge is good. But I need to hear Your thoughts. Learning to quiet myself and listen to that still, small voice isn't my first inclination, Father. Thank You for the reminder that You've got answers to whisper in my ear, things yet to be revealed. Amen.

. . . .

These are the things God has revealed to us by his Spirit. The Spirit searches all things, even the deep things of God. For who knows a person's thoughts except their own spirit within them? In the same way no one knows the thoughts of God except the Spirit of God.

1 Corinthians 2:10–11 NIV

A Generous Supply

God, there is no creature on earth You do not see or provide for. I'm bringing praise to You right now for the daily things You supply for me. It is through Your goodness that I have food to eat, clothes to wear, and water to drink. Help me always be thankful for what I have and not emulate the wandering Israelites who, focusing on lack, preferred to complain. Your power is awesome; thank You for generously supplying my needs each and every day. Amen.

* *

*You open Your hand and satisfy
the desire of every living thing.*
PSALM 145:16 NKJV

Coveting

God, it's so easy to break the tenth commandment: Do not covet (see Exodus 20:17). Coveting is a way of life for many in our world. But You say we shouldn't compare ourselves with the "Joneses" nor envy them and what they have. Whatever You've given me is to be enjoyed and received, not held up for inspection. Teach me a deeper gratefulness for Your blessings. In Jesus' name, amen.

. . . .

Let your conduct be without covetousness.
HEBREWS 13:5 NKJV

Perfect Holiness

God, when I consider my own inadequacies, I am amazed at Your perfectness. You are truth and justice, holiness and integrity. There is none like You. You are the one and only true God. Other deities disappoint their followers; other idols fail. But You never do. Because You are perfect holiness, all Your other attributes are only good. There is no selfishness, vengefulness, or deceitfulness in You, Lord. Thus, I can trust You completely and revel in Your light unafraid. Amen.

* *

"No one is holy like the LORD, for there is none besides You, nor is there any rock like our God."

1 SAMUEL 2:2 NKJV

Peace, Please

Dear Jesus, someone I love dearly is in the hospital. I'm sitting here in the busy waiting room, watching for the doctor, wanting news, and yet dreading to hear it. Others surround me, connected to this place by a person they care about. We're people from every stratum and season of life with one thing in common—knowing someone who is suffering physically. Lord, illness and injury have to obey Your will, and so do the emotions that burden the hearts of those here. Please visit every waiting area and patient's room, and bring the cure that only comes from You—tranquility, mercy, and courage. Amen.

. . . .

Now the God of peace be with you all.
ROMANS 15:33 NKJV

No Hiding

All things are visible to You, Father. Your kids don't get away with shenanigans because You're an all-seeing God. We are like babes on the changing table, naked and bare before You. There's not a thing about us You don't know: our angst, bitterness, concerns, joys. But You don't leave us to wallow in our woes, Father. (Thank goodness!) Just as a mother changes her child, You are ready to step in and change our hearts. Praise You for seeking us out, Lord. Amen.

. . . .

Neither is there any creature that is not manifest in his sight: but all things are naked and opened unto the eyes of him with whom we have to do.

HEBREWS 4:13 KJV

Demonstrating Love

God, I have the most demanding boss ever. I need to demonstrate the love of Christ, but it can be challenging when my superior is, at times, so hard to please. Give me courage, Lord, to rise above my emotions. Help me to pray for my boss as the Bible tells me to and to serve as though it is an assignment from You. For You, Lord, are my true superior. Bless my boss today, God, and show Your love to him through me. Amen.

. . . .

Whatever you do, work at it with all your heart,
as working for the Lord, not for human masters.
COLOSSIANS 3:23 NIV

The Same Old Me

Lord, today I come to You a bit discouraged. The traits I see in myself are ones I don't like. It seems I could do much more for You without some of the inherent flaws of my personality. So help me overcome my defects—or use me in spite of them. Help me to love myself, as imperfect as I am, and to strive to be the best me I can be. I know You can find a way around my impediments and use me for Your glory, just like You used Moses in spite of his speech problem. Amen.

. . . .

You have searched me, LORD, and you know me.
PSALM 139:1 NIV

A Sense of Purpose

Father, I'm in a rut. I like some familiarity, but this monotony is wearing away at my sense of purpose. I know there are parts of our lives that are not particularly glamorous, fulfilling, or significant (at least, on the surface). Yet living without passion or purpose isn't what You had in mind for us. Show me, Lord, how to find meaning in my everyday life. Open up to my eyes the subtle nuances of joy folded into life's mundane hours. I put my longings into Your hands. Amen.

* *

In Him also we have obtained an inheritance, being predestined according to the purpose of Him who works all things according to the counsel of His will.
EPHESIANS 1:11 NKJV

DAY 328

One Nation Under God

Dear God, I am so weary of the bickering in our nation. It disturbs me to see people attempting to remove You from schools, courtrooms, and anywhere else they think of. They distort history and deny that this nation was founded with You as her leader. Heal us, Lord. Help us return to You! Amen.

. . . .

I am the light of the world: he that followeth me shall not walk in darkness, but shall have the light of life.
JOHN 8:12 KJV

Your Counsel Stands

Because You see all and know all, You can be trusted with not just my life but my family, my community, my state, my country—the whole of humankind, in fact. When the news on TV is bad, I can trust You, Father. When things are falling apart politically, You're still on the throne. You know best how to reach the hearts of those who need change, Father. Help me release any anxieties and rest in the knowledge that You know and You care. Your counsel stands, Lord. How mighty You are! Amen.

. . . .

Declaring the end from the beginning, and from ancient times the things that are not yet done, saying, My counsel shall stand, and I will do all my pleasure.
Isaiah 46:10 kjv

DAY 330

Think on Pure Things

There's just not much in today's society that encourages purity, but Your Word certainly demonstrates the importance of focusing our attention upon things that are pure. From experience, I have learned that life is more satisfying when it's geared toward pleasing You rather than the flesh, and I thank You for these lessons. Amen.

. . . .

Ye shall walk after the LORD your God, and fear him, and keep his commandments, and obey his voice, and ye shall serve him, and cleave unto him.

DEUTERONOMY 13:4 KJV

Blank Stares

Today, I'm struggling, Jesus. I have a specific goal that needs to be met, but it requires clarity of mind. The project is spread out before me, but I'm staring at it blankly. I know You want me to work on it, and I need Your guidance. Give me the ability to think and complete the task. Amen.

. . . .

In all thy ways acknowledge him,
and he shall direct thy paths.
PROVERBS 3:6 KJV

Confidante

Dear God, the Bible tells older women to mentor younger women. That's an element missing from my life. Although my mom did a great job of passing along the life lessons she'd learned and we have a good relationship, I still need the insight and affirmation of an older woman. Lord, I need a trusted confidante, one who will help me succeed. I ask You to send someone like that my way in fulfillment of Your Word. And let me fill that role myself someday when I have the required résumé. Amen.

. . . .

May [the aged women] teach the young women to be sober, to love their husbands, to love their children.

TITUS 2:4 KJV

Gentle Peace

Thank You, Lord, for this opportunity to bask in the peace that You offer. As I sit here in the woods, listening to the creek gently bubbling over the stones, I am reminded how Your presence in my life soothes even in the midst of chaos. I'm glad I have Your peace! Amen.

. . . .

The LORD bless thee, and keep thee: the LORD make his face shine upon thee, and be gracious unto thee: the LORD lift up his countenance upon thee, and give thee peace.
NUMBERS 6:24–26 KJV

A Light on My Path

I know what it's like to stumble around in the dark, Lord. Toes get stubbed. Knees get bumped. Things get knocked over. Sure, my eyes adjust to a certain extent, but I'm still second-guessing myself because things aren't as clear as they should be. I can't make out the road signs. But You provide a light, Father. When I'm feeling unsure, I ask You to brighten my path so that I don't cause damage as I move along. I'm glad You illuminate the road for me, Lord. I praise You for that. Amen.

. . . .

Your word is a lamp for my feet,
a light on my path.
Psalm 119:105 NIV

Instant Gratification

Dear Lord, so many things are instantaneous in my world. From fast food to instant credit, we can satisfy our penchant for immediate gratification at every juncture. But I have to keep reminding myself that You often work by process. When it comes to the work You're doing in me, You use the steady maturing of Your Word within me to make me more like Jesus. You, the master gardener, water the seeds, prune the unnecessary limbs, and watch over me carefully as the fruit of my life continues to ripen. Instead of being impatient, I aim to revel in Your timely and tender loving care. Amen.

. . . .

But grow in grace, and in the knowledge
of our Lord and Saviour Jesus Christ.
2 Peter 3:18 kjv

Golden Words Needed

Heavenly Father, today I need affirming words. You know that words are important to me as a woman. You also know that I struggle with self-worth. The other people in my world don't always meet my need to be affirmed verbally, and I can't expect them to fulfill every void in my life. So, Lord, let me look to and in Your Word to find the love and encouragement I need. In Jesus' name, amen.

. . . .

A word fitly spoken is like apples of gold in settings of silver.
PROVERBS 25:11 NKJV

Letting Go of Bitterness

Bitterness is like cancer, God. It grows and takes over, squeezing out life. I don't want to be marked or consumed by bitterness. Let me not hold to the injustices I've experienced. Help me accept Your healing touch and let go of the beginnings of bitterness in my soul. As Joseph noted in the Old Testament, You can turn things meant for evil into good. Please do that in my life. In Christ's name, amen.

. . . .

Let all bitterness, wrath, anger,
clamor, and evil speaking be put
away from you, with all malice.
EPHESIANS 4:31 NKJV

DAY 338

For Each New Day

Every day there is something for which I can offer You praise, dear God! To begin with, we have the promise of a fresh start—a new opportunity to serve You. Throughout the day You show Your majesty in a multitude of ways. You are an awesome God! Amen.

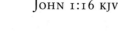

And of his fulness have all we
received, and grace for grace.
JOHN 1:16 KJV

Made from the Invisible

Life is like a giant puzzle to me at times, Lord; only the puzzle pieces aren't always clear. Sometimes I feel like I'm groping around in the dark, trying to force things together. I can't always get the pieces to fit. Oh, but You have the perfect plan all prepared in advance. There's no need to force anything, is there? What I can't see, You can. When I can't fit the invisible pieces together, You shuffle the board in Your own creative way and make things crystal clear so that I only move when I feel led by Your Spirit. Trusting when my vision isn't clear isn't always easy, but You make it worth it, Father. Thank You! Amen.

. . . .

By faith we understand that the universe
was formed at God's command, so that what
is seen was not made out of what was visible.

HEBREWS 11:3 NIV

DAY 340
Today!

Father in heaven, I have a tendency to try to live a week or month at a time. It's difficult for me to limit myself to one day, one hour, one minute. But that's how You want me to live. You know that projecting into the future causes me to wonder and worry about things that haven't happened yet. You also know that I can't be any good to anyone if my head is in the clouds, thinking about the future. So help me live in today—it's all I have at the moment. Amen.

* *

"Does He not see my ways, and count all my steps?"
JOB 31:4 NKJV

DAY 341

Poise

Heavenly Father, I need poise—that kind of gracious manner and behavior that characterized women of past generations. It seems to be disdained in my culture. Women now are expected and encouraged to be free spirits—unrestricted by convention and decorum. But I cringe when I observe women using crude language, slouching in their seats, and adopting careless ways of walking and eating. I don't want to seem prissy and uppity, but I do want to guard against being too informal. Help me develop the traits that portray womanhood as the gentle, beautiful, fascinating gender You designed. Amen.

. . . .

Like a gold ring in a pig's snout is a
beautiful woman who shows no discretion.

Proverbs 11:22 niv

DAY 342

Claim Peace

Father, peace is an elusive emotion. So many people talk about peace, but few can claim it. You promised to give us Your peace, a calm assurance that You are present and sovereign in all our ways. I want more of this peace every day. Although there are many upsetting things in my world, Your peace will help me cope with them all. Amid Your peace, I am neither troubled nor afraid, merely allowing myself to bask in Your presence. Amen.

. . . .

"Peace I leave with you,
My peace I give to you."
JOHN 14:27 NKJV

New Compassions

I really didn't want to get up this morning, Father. My blankets seemed like good protection from the cares of the day. But when I saw the glorious sunrise and heard the cheerful, singing birds, I was reminded that Your compassions are new every morning. I knew everything would be fine. Thank You for Your faithfulness.

. . . .

Sing unto the LORD, bless his name;
shew forth his salvation from day to day.

PSALM 96:2 KJV

With All My Heart

Here's a little confession, Lord: I often do things half-heartedly. Housework. Laundry. Tasks at my job. This is difficult to admit, but I don't always give my relationship with You 100 percent, either. Of course, You already know that. You see my motivation (or lack thereof). I'm so sorry, Father. It feels good to make that confession because I want to be an "all-in" sort of girl, one who seeks You with my whole heart. Give me the push I need, even when I don't feel like it, Lord. Amen.

* *

"Then you will call on me and come and pray to me, and I will listen to you. You will seek me and find me when you seek me with all your heart."

JEREMIAH 29:12–13 NIV

From the Mountain

Lord, it feels good to be alive! When I got out of bed this morning, I had this wonderful sense of well-being. Some days I awaken with something negative on my mind, some trouble on the horizon, or some ache in my body. But today, I feel great in mind, spirit, and body. This road of life has both mountains and valleys. But right now, I'm going to enjoy the mountain— the brightness, the beauty, and the refreshing that will help me face any challenge that comes my way today or tomorrow. I love You, Lord. Thank You for good surprises!

* *

Oh, give thanks to the LORD, for He is good! For His mercy endures forever.
PSALM 107:1 NKJV

Lessons in Trust

Heavenly Father, teach me to trust. I know it's an area of weakness for me. In spite of the fact that I know Your character and Your track record, I find it so difficult to relinquish to You the important areas of life. Oh, I say that I will, and I do put forth effort to rely on You, but we both know that, in my heart, I find it hard to let You handle everything. So take my hand, Lord, and teach me to trust. You're the Master; I am forever Your student. In Christ's name, amen.

. . . .

I have put my trust in the Lord God,
that I may declare all Your works.
PSALM 73:28 NKJV

When I'm Not Prepared

Father God, I've put myself in a bind because I procrastinated. I knew this was looming ahead of me, but I wanted to do other things first. Or, at least, I wanted to leave the task until the right time. But now, there is no more time, and I'm not prepared. Please help me, Lord, working all things to my good. Amen.

. . . .

Make the most of every opportunity.
EPHESIANS 5:16 NLT

Yet to Be Revealed

My vision is so cloudy at times, Lord. I can't see what's coming around the next bend, let alone where You're taking me in this coming season of my life. (Oh, how I wish I could!) Trusting You when I can't see is a bit like walking on water. I don't always have the security of knowing that my eyes won't deceive me, and sometimes I feel like I'm going under. But I know I can trust You, Father. You haven't let me drown yet. I'll keep my eyes on You, Lord. Amen.

- -

Dear friends, now we are children of God,
and what we will be has not yet been made
known. But we know that when Christ appears,
we shall be like him, for we shall see him as he is.
1 JOHN 3:2 NIV

All-Seeing

My vision is so limited, Father. I can only see what's right in front of me. (And sometimes—especially when I'm looking for something specific, like my keys or phone—I can't even see what's right in front of me.) I certainly can't see what's happening one street over or in another city, yet You see all. You are witness to every action, every word, every thought. Because You see, I can trust You, Lord. Oh, how blessed I am that my heavenly Father has twenty-twenty vision! Amen.

* * *

The eyes of the LORD are everywhere,
keeping watch on the wicked and the good.
PROVERBS 15:3 NIV

He's in Control

Thank You, Lord, that You have a perfect plan for my life. I know I don't always understand it, but You know what's best, and everything that happens is for a reason—that You might be glorified. I'm so glad that You are in control and that I need not worry. Amen.

. . . .

There are many devices in a man's heart;
nevertheless the counsel of the LORD, that shall stand.
PROVERBS 19:21 KJV

Special Instructions

Thank You for Your Word, Father. Without it, I would be a helpless cause in regard to developing godly character. I'm so glad You preserved these special words that give me specific instruction on how to live. Help me to hide these scriptures in my heart so that I'm able to rely on them throughout my life. Amen.

. . . .

Thy word is a lamp unto my feet,
and a light unto my path.
PSALM 119:105 KJV

DAY 352

You Made the Day

When I ponder the fact that time is in Your hands and that You created days, hours, minutes, and seconds, I realize that each and every nanosecond is Yours to do with as You please. If You created these things, they are Yours to manage. I don't have to fret over the items on my to-do list that don't get done today, Father. All I ask is that You—my perfect, all-knowing Father— guide my steps. I will do my best to rejoice in this day, Lord, and to be happy knowing You are in control and I'm not. (Whew, what a relief!) Amen.

* *

This is the day the LORD has made.
We will rejoice and be glad in it.

PSALM 118:24 NLT

DAY 353
Full to the Brim

Father, what an amazing picture You have painted with this verse. Your knowledge is too lofty for me. I cannot attain it. But I can picture it spread out like mighty rushing waters across this planet, covering vast areas. My thoughts hardly compare to Yours. They are minute in comparison. But You invite me to share glimpses, to see that Your ways—though higher—are better for me than my own. How could I not trust a God who sees all, knows all, and guides all? I trust You, Lord. Amen.

* * *

*For the earth shall be full of the knowledge
of the Lord, as the waters cover the sea.*
Isaiah 11:9 kjv

You Know the Heart

Only You know the motivations of others, Lord. I question people all the time—wondering where their hearts are, wondering why they do the things they do. Why they choose to hurt others. Why they fall down on the job. Why they don't follow through. Why they break promises. It's not mine to question, Father, but to trust that You will speak to the deepest places in their hearts. I can trust You to know what's going on, deep inside each of us. I praise You for that! Amen.

* * *

"Forgive and act; deal with everyone according to all they do, since you know their hearts (for you alone know every human heart), so that they will fear you all the time they live in the land you gave our ancestors."
1 KINGS 8:39–40 NIV

Divine Guidance

Dear Lord, it's so hard sometimes to know what Your will is. You don't write specific instructions in the sky nor emblazon them on a marquee. So how can I know exactly what You want me to do? How can I keep from making a big mistake? How can I proceed with this decision? I ask today that You would give me wisdom; please send me guidance as I seek Your will. Through a person, a thought, a scripture, let me sense Your leading for this situation. I want my life to honor Your plan for me. In Christ's name, amen.

. . . .

If any of you lacks wisdom, you should ask God, who gives generously to all without finding fault, and it will be given to you.

JAMES 1:5 NIV

Christ Jesus My Intercessor

Jesus, You went to the cross, spent time in hell, and rose from the grave in order to bring me back into relationship with the Father. You did not come to condemn me but to give me eternal life. When Satan condemns me or accuses me, remind me that You are my advocate. You go before me interceding for me. You make a way when there seems to be no way. You understand when no one else does. You bring me up from the messes I find myself in. You are always on my side, giving me hope and a reason to press on.

• •

Who is he who condemns? It is Christ who died, and furthermore is also risen, who is even at the right hand of God, who also makes intercession for us.

ROMANS 8:34 NKJV

DAY 357

Perfectly Knit

When I ponder the fact that Your work in my life began even before You knit me together in my mother's womb, I'm floored, Father. You thought this out, long before I came into being. You went to so much trouble just to make me who I am. You know everything about, well, everything—and that brings such comfort. I know I can trust You, my Creator, to guide me every step of the way. Amen.

- -

*You have searched me, Lord, and you know
me. You know when I sit and when I rise; you
perceive my thoughts from afar. You discern my
going out and my lying down; you are familiar
with all my ways. . . . Such knowledge is too
wonderful for me, too lofty for me to attain.*
PSALM 139:1–3, 6 NIV

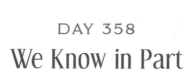

We Know in Part

I'll admit it, Lord—there have been times in my life when I've acted like a know-it-all. I've tried to show up others or prove they were wrong and I was right. I must confess that I don't know it all, Father. Only You can claim that. I know in part. You know in full. It boggles my mind to think about the scope of Your knowledge, especially when it comes to the plans You've made for my life. I trust not in what I do or don't know but in You, the All-Knowing. You've got me covered, Father. Bless You for that! Amen.

For now we see only a reflection as in a mirror; then we shall see face to face. Now I know in part; then I shall know fully, even as I am fully known.

1 CORINTHIANS 13:12 NIV

You Look at My Heart

Lord, it troubles me to see how much interest people put in outward appearance. Clothing. Shoes. Make-up. Hairstyles. These things are fine, but when they become the focus—the primary things people notice—something is amiss. I'm so glad You're not examining me from the outside in, making sure I measure up to society's standards. Thank You for looking at my heart. Not that my heart is perfect, as You well know, but You're so good at ironing out the wrinkles when things are off-kilter internally. What a gracious God You are. Amen.

. . . .

But the LORD said to Samuel, "Do not consider his appearance or his height, for I have rejected him. The LORD does not look at the things people look at. People look at the outward appearance, but the LORD looks at the heart."

1 SAMUEL 16:7 NIV

Things Not Seen

Jesus, it is easy to believe in that which I can see. I wish I could reach out and touch You. As I meditate on Your Word, give me faith in that which I cannot see. Give me faith that all of Your promises are true and that one day You will come again in the clouds to take me home. Amen.

. . . .

Now faith is the substance of things hoped for, the evidence of things not seen.
HEBREWS 11:1 KJV

In the Waves

Lord, I am like Peter walking to You on the waves. You tell me to take courage and to not be afraid. You tell me to come to You, and I step out of my boat of comfort, of stability. I am so confident and sure of Your power until I focus on the darkness around me, the heartache, and my own sin. Before I know it, I falter. I sink faster every moment I don't trust Your ways. Forgive me for taking my eyes off You. Forgive me for trying to do things on my own instead of letting You lead. I thank You for always catching me when I fall, for pulling me from the water and the waves of life. Today, Lord, I ask You to help me rely on the truth that I can stand firm in my faith during storms because You are for me.

*Immediately Jesus reached out his hand
and caught him. "You of little faith,"
he said, "why did you doubt?"*
MATTHEW 14:31 NIV

My Deliverance

You are my Deliverer. The heavy weight of life's challenges brings me to my knees, at the throne of Your grace. Thoughts of defeat overwhelm me, and yet I remember the Israelites standing between the Egyptians and the Red Sea. Their oppressors were closing in fast, and fear of returning to captivity pressed in. Miraculously, You parted the sea and made a way of escape for them. You will do the same for me. Nothing is impossible for You. You will show me the way out in Your time. I trust that my deliverance is on its way.

* *

Moses spoke to the people: "Don't be afraid. Stand firm and watch GOD do his work of salvation for you today. Take a good look at the Egyptians today for you're never going to see them again."

EXODUS 14:13 MSG

A Glimpse Inside

I'm so grateful for the times when You pull back the curtain, Lord, and give me tiny glimpses into Your plans for my life. I can hardly comprehend the magnificence of Your thought process, but Your love is overwhelming during these "glimpsing" seasons. What a privilege to walk through life with Your hand so tightly clasped in my own. What a joy to know that I can trust You implicitly. And how generous and kind You are, Lord. All You ask is that I call on You. So today, I choose to do that with my whole heart. Amen.

. . . .

"Call to me and I will answer you and tell you great and unsearchable things you do not know."
JEREMIAH 33:3 NIV

Like-Minded with My Father

I don't always know or understand Your thoughts, Lord; but I am created in Your image, which gives me glimpses into Your will for my life. Thank You for giving me the mind of Christ. What a privilege, to be like-minded with You, Lord! May my heart beat in sync with Yours, and may my thought life respond as You guide my every step. Amen.

. . . .

Then God said, "Let us make human beings in our image, to be like us. They will reign over the fish in the sea, the birds in the sky, the livestock, all the wild animals on the earth, and the small animals that scurry along the ground."

GENESIS 1:26 NLT

God Is Faithful

God, I focus a lot on my faith in You. And then, You show me that it is not all about me. You are faithful to me. You show me how to be faithful. You never leave. You never give up on me. You never turn away. You always show up. You always believe in me. You are faithful by Your very nature. You cannot be unfaithful. Thank You for Your faithfulness in my life. Amen.

But the Lord is faithful, who shall stablish you, and keep you from evil.
2 Thessalonians 3:3 kjv

Scripture Index

OLD TESTAMENT

Genesis

1:1	Day 214
1:26	Day 364

Exodus

14:13	Day 362
14:14	Day 178
20:12	Day 170
33:11	Day 26
33:14	Day 271

Numbers

6:24-26	Day 333
23:19	Day 180

Deuteronomy

5:16	Day 73
8:18	Day 119
13:4	Day 330
26:11	Day 83
31:6	Day 19, 176
31:8	Day 162

Joshua

1:8	Day 22, 96, 202
1:9	Day 217

1 Samuel

2:2	Day 322
16:7	Day 359
30:6	Day 250

2 SAMUEL

7:18. . . . . Day 171

1 KINGS

8:39–40. . . . . Day 354

2 CHRONICLES

16:9. . . . . Day 200

NEHEMIAH

8:10. . . . . Day 12

ESTHER

2:15. . . . . Day 152

JOB

5:9. . . . . Day 44, 66

11:18. . . . . Day 36

12:13. . . . . Day 201

12:22. . . . . Day 6

23:10. . . . . Day 75

28:10. . . . . Day 203

28:24. . . . . Day 1

31:4. . . . . Day 229, 340

33:4. . . . . Day 77

34:21. . . . . Day 195

37:16. . . . . Day 210

PSALMS

3:2–6. . . . . Day 39

5:11. . . . . Day 220

16:5. . . . . Day 144

17:8. . . . . Day 216

17:15. . . . . Day 189

18:30, 34–35 . . . . Day 199

19:7–8. . . . . Day 58

23:1–3. . . . . Day 79
23:3. . . . . Day 190
23:4. . . . . Day 155, 246
25:4. . . . . Day 193
27:4. . . . . Day 315
32:1. . . . . Day 226
33:4. . . . . Day 230
34:18. . . . . Day 82
37:4. . . . . Day 245
37:7. . . . . Introduction
37:25–26. . . . . Day 274
39:7. . . . . Day 308
40:3. . . . . Day 282
42:5. . . . . Day 15
46:10. . . . . Day 181
50:10. . . . . Day 183
55:22. . . . . Day 293
62:5–6. . . . . Day 95
62:11–12. . . . . Day 145
73:28. . . . . Day 346
80:18–19. . . . . Day 167
90:12. . . . . Day 296
91:14–16. . . . . Day 97
92:2. . . . . Day 153
94:18–19. . . . . Day 55
94:19. . . . . Day 290
96:2. . . . . Day 343
103:13. . . . . Day 138
107:1. . . . . Day 345
107:13–16. . . . . Day 169
112:4. . . . . Day 286
113:5. . . . . Day 4
118:24. . . . . Day 242, 352

119:1. . . . . Day 90
119:10–11. . . . . Day 45
119:30. . . . . Day 291
119:40. . . . . Day 31
119:105. . . . . Day 334, 351
119:106–107. . . . . Day 60
119:111–112. . . . . Day 63
119:114. . . . . Day 74
119:129–130. . . . . Day 85
127:1. . . . . Day 225
131:3. . . . . Day 100
133:2. . . . . Day 139
138:3. . . . . Day 163
138:8. . . . . Day 136
139:1. . . . . Day 326
139:1–3, 6. . . . . Day 357
139:2–3. . . . . Day 288
139:6. . . . . Day 228
139:13–14. . . . . Day 260
139:15–16. . . . . Day 244
143:8. . . . . Day 118, 231
145:16. . . . . Day 68, 320
146:5. . . . . Day 53
147:4. . . . . Day 235

PROVERBS

3:3. . . . . Day 266
3:5. . . . . Day 280
3:5–6. . . . . Day 148, 259
3:6. . . . . Day 331
3:19–20. . . . . Day 205
4:11. . . . . Day 270
4:20–22. . . . . Day 34
6:27. . . . . Day 253

8:11. . . . . Day 263
9:10. . . . . Day 179
10:12. . . . . Day 292
10:19. . . . . Day 265
10:28. . . . . Day 89
11:2. . . . . Day 278
11:22. . . . . Day 341
12:26. . . . . Day 219
15:3. . . . . Day 349
15:19. . . . . Day 168
17:17. . . . . Day 248
18:10. . . . . Day 76
18:21. . . . . Day 301
19:20. . . . . Day 166, 269
19:21. . . . . Day 350
24:14. . . . . Day 29
25:11. . . . . Day 336
27:17. . . . . Day 98
31:27. . . . . Day 78
31:30. . . . . Day 275

ECCLESIASTES

3:11. . . . . Day 35
4:9–10. . . . . Day 93
5:10 . . . . Day 194
9:10. . . . . Day 172

ISAIAH

11:9. . . . . Day 353
26:3. . . . . Day 91
29:15–16. . . . . Day 206
30:21. . . . . Day 154
40:29. . . . . Day 131
40:31. . . . . Day 123

41:4. . . . . Day 209
41:10. . . . . Day 314
41:13. . . . . Day 9
43:2. . . . . Day 161, 213
46:4. . . . . Day 221
46:10. . . . . Day 329
49:16. . . . . Day 309
55:8. . . . . Day 177
55:11. . . . . Day 84
55:12–13. . . . . Day 135
60:1–2. . . . . Day 94
61:1. . . . . Day 87

JEREMIAH
10:23. . . . . Day 307
17:7. . . . . Day 40
29:11. . . . . Day 303
29:12–13. . . . . Day 344
30:17. . . . . Day 46
31:33. . . . . Day 164
33:3. . . . . Day 363
33:6. . . . . Day 42
51:15. . . . . Day 208

LAMENTATIONS
3:22–23. . . . . Day 156

EZEKIEL
22:30. . . . . Day 61

DANIEL
1:8. . . . . Day 17
12:3. . . . . Day 186

AMOS
9:13. . . . . Day 130

MICAH

6:8. . . . . Day 92

HABAKKUK

1:5. . . . . Day 127

ZEPHANIAH

3:17. . . . . Day 51, 310

MALACHI

3:10. . . . . Day 281

NEW TESTAMENT

MATTHEW

5:14–16. . . . . Day 243

5:16. . . . . Day 204

5:46–47. . . . . Day 305

6:24. . . . . Day 38, 317

6:31–32. . . . . Day 65, 218

6:33. . . . . Day 140, 239

7:9–11. . . . . Day 114

9:22. . . . . Day 237

10:30. . . . . Day 240

11:28. . . . . Day 236

11:29–30. . . . . Day 252

14:30–31. . . . . Day 105

14:31. . . . . Day 361

15:28. . . . . Day 233

19:26. . . . . Day 86

24:35. . . . . Day 47

26:8–10. . . . . Day 110

28:18. . . . . Day 197

28:19. . . . . Day 249

28:20. . . . . Day 185

MARK

6:31. . . . . Day 227
6:50–51. . . . . Day 2
8:35. . . . . Day 62
9:23–24. . . . . Day 14
12:30. . . . . Day 289

LUKE

6:38. . . . . Day 261
8:25. . . . . Day 72
10:36–37. . . . . Day 222
11:9. . . . . Day 191
12:25–26. . . . . Day 59
12:32. . . . . Day 175
15:9. . . . . Day 188

JOHN

1:16. . . . . Day 338
3:16. . . . . Day 182
3:17. . . . . Day 117
5:6. . . . . Day 37
8:12. . . . . Day 328
8:36. . . . . Day 165
8:44. . . . . Day 106
10:14. . . . . Day 198
11:41–42. . . . . Day 69
14:2–3. . . . . Day 264
14:21. . . . . Day 295
14:26. . . . . Day 56, 283
14:27. . . . . Day 111, 113, 342
15:11. . . . . Day 18, 277
16:22. . . . . Day 23
16:33. . . . . Day 212

Acts

1:7. . . . . Day 294
1:8. . . . . Day 255
2:24. . . . . Day 150
2:28. . . . . Day 27
3:6. . . . . Day 128
17:28. . . . . Day 285
20:35. . . . . Day 49, 257

Romans

5:2–5. . . . . Day 33
6:23. . . . . Day 80
8:11. . . . . Day 137
8:27. . . . . Day 64
8:28. . . . . Day 143
8:34. . . . . Day 356
8:38–39. . . . . Day 20, 107
10:9–10. . . . . Day 158
11:33. . . . . Day 247
11:33–34. . . . . Day 173
12:12. . . . . Day 24
12:18–19. . . . . Day 223
13:12. . . . . Day 124
15:13. . . . . Day 3, 129
15:33. . . . . Day 323

1 Corinthians

2:9–10. . . . . Day 146
2:10–11. . . . . Day 319
6:18. . . . . Day 256
10:13. . . . . Day 11
10:31. . . . . Day 43, 316
12:18. . . . . Day 224
13:8. . . . . Day 272

13:12. . . . . Day 358

15:10 . . . . Day 71

15:57–58. . . . . Day 192

15:58. . . . . Day 81

2 CORINTHIANS

1:3–4. . . . . Day 160

4:17–18. . . . . Day 159

5:17. . . . . Day 28

GALATIANS

2:20. . . . . Day 184

5:13–14. . . . . Day 57

5:22–23. . . . . Day 133

6:9. . . . . Day 238

EPHESIANS

1:7. . . . . Day 13

1:11. . . . . Day 327

1:18. . . . . Day 16

2:8. . . . . Day 21

2:8–9. . . . . Day 297

3:14–16. . . . . Day 268

3:19. . . . . Day 215

3:20–21. . . . . Day 112

4:2. . . . . Day 267

4:11–12. . . . . Day 88

4:14–15. . . . . Day 99

4:22–24. . . . . Day 151

4:31. . . . . Day 306, 337

5:8–9. . . . . Day 109

5:16. . . . . Day 347

6:6–7. . . . . Day 234

6:12. . . . . Day 103

6:16. . . . . Day 104

PHILIPPIANS

1:6. . . . . Day 187
2:12–13. . . . . Day 157
2:17–18. . . . . Day 102
4:6. . . . . Day 5
4:7. . . . . Day 48
4:8. . . . . .Day 50, 108, 311
4:11. . . . . Day 142
4:13. . . . . Day 241
4:19. . . . . Day 122, 211

COLOSSIANS

3:13. . . . . Day 174
3:15. . . . . Day 287
3:23. . . . . Day 325
3:23–24. . . . . Day 32

1 THESSALONIANS

2:13. . . . . Day 67
4:11. . . . . Day 258
5:8–10. . . . . Day 54
5:16–18. . . . . Day 52, 115

2 THESSALONIANS

3:3. . . . . Day 365

1 TIMOTHY

2:3–4. . . . . Day 304
2:9–10. . . . . Day 318

TITUS

2:4 . . . . Day 332
2:11. . . . . Day 132
3:7. . . . . Day 25, 302

HEBREWS

4:12 . . . . Day 196
4:13 . . . . Day 324
10:36 . . . . Day 299
11:1 . . . . Day 360
11:3 . . . . Day 339
11:6 . . . . Day 134
12:1 . . . . Day 251
13:5 . . . . Day 321

JAMES

1:2–3 . . . . Day 10
1:5 . . . . Day 355
1:17 . . . . Day 120
1:22 . . . . Day 254
4:3 . . . . Day 70
4:6 . . . . Day 8

1 PETER

1:21 . . . . Day 30
3:3–4 . . . . Day 121
3:8 . . . . Day 279
3:9 . . . . Day 284
3:15–16 . . . . Day 41
4:9 . . . . Day 276
4:10 . . . . Day 300
5:8 . . . . Day 232

2 PETER

1:4 . . . . Day 207
1:5–7 . . . . Day 298
2:9 . . . . Day 273
3:18 . . . . Day 335

1 JOHN

3:2... Day 348
3:17.. Day 126
3:18.. Day 312
3:19–20...................................... Day 7
3:19–21...................................... Day 149
5:14.. Day 262

3 JOHN

1:2... Day 116

JUDE

1:20–21....................................... Day 141
1:22–23....................................... Day 125

REVELATION

5:11–12....................................... Day 313
15:4.. Day 101
21:1.. Day 147